Life in the Hand
of an Extraordinary
God

Seeing God in the Everyday

Elizabeth,
May you always live in
awe of God's great love
for you. Blessings,
Sue Nygren

Isaiah 41:13

Life in the Hand of an Extraordinary God

Seeing God in the Everyday

Susan Nystrom

Cover and illustrations by
Loren Nystrom

In loving memory
of my parents
Pete and Virginia Donohue
whose love will remain
forever in my heart

and

Jeff Kinbacher
who taught me that it is normal
to hear the voice of God

CONTENTS

ACKNOWLEDGMENTS

No book is ever written and truly complete without the help of special people who come alongside to encourage and contribute their gifts and talents. I am grateful to many, but must acknowledge a few before the story can be told.

To my wonderful husband, Loren: Thank you for lending your genius to this book. The cover and illustrations capture the essence of the message in simple beauty, much like our life together. Your dedication to learn and to do the work of putting this book together has been such a blessing to me, and I couldn't have done it without you. We have taken this journey together, as one, and I am honored to walk by your side. I love you.

To our adult children, Keith and Cheryl: Oh, how I thank God for the privilege of being your mother. Thank you for allowing me to open a window into our lives and share some of the lessons I have learned from you. I am so proud of the man and woman you have become. Thanks for sharing this dream with me. Always remember, I love you and Jesus loves you.

To Michelle Nystrom and Jim Ball: Thank you for loving Keith and Cheryl so well. You are both a true blessing to this family and your encouragements have meant the world to me.

To our grandchildren, CJ and Lexi: You bring so much joy into my life. Thanks for praying, playing and using your imagination with me. CJ, I thank you for being the first person ever to call me an author. You bestowed a great honor on me that day. And sweet Lexi, I thank you for always believing in me. Though only five years old, you once told me, "You don't need to change any words. You write well!" I can't wait until you can read!

To my soul mate, Maria Fischer: Thank you for your steadfast belief that this book would one day become a reality and for covering it and me so faithfully in prayer through the years. We have walked this path together, my friend, and your love and friendship have been one of God's greatest blessings in my life.

To my sister Janice Donohue Spillan: Thank you for the sacrificial gift of time and energy, beautifully wrapped in patience and love, as you spent countless hours transcribing this book from my handwritten manuscript. Thank you for always listening with your heart and for laughing and crying in all the right places. I love you, my sister, my friend.

To Catherine Hurst Alexandrow, Jane Campbell, Jeannine Cotner and Duane Nystrom: In spite of Lexi's confidence, it actually took four very insightful people to edit this story. Thank you for your enthusiasm, encouragement and helpful suggestions in making this a better book. Each of you brought a special touch from the Lord. I am enormously grateful.

To my friend and confidante Barbara Day: Thank you for making it a pleasure to go to work every day. We made a great team. But, more importantly, we make great friends. Your laughter comes from a vast storehouse of joy that is contagious. When I couldn't imagine going off to a "writing cabin in the woods," you provided a "writing condo in the suburbs." You, my dear sister in the Lord, are beautiful and greatly loved.

To the Reverend David Harper: Thank you for your spiritual guidance and friendship through the years and for teaching us by example how to listen and obey the voice of God.

To those who know they are an important part of my life but don't appear in this book: Don't worry. Your name is written in the only Book that truly matters. I love and appreciate you.

To you, the reader: Thank you for embarking on this journey with me. May you discover God's hand on your own life as you travel through these pages. If this book proves to be a blessing to you, I hope you will share it with others who need to know that God sees them and cares.

And to the Author of life: Thank You for never letting go of my hand. You are an awesome, extraordinary and extravagant God in all You do. Thank You for leading me on this path of a grace-filled life. All the glory and honor belong to You. "I love You, O LORD, my strength" (Psalm 18:1).

LETTER TO THE READER

Dear fellow traveler,

We are all on a journey called life. Our walks take us in many different directions, but the destination is the same. Jesus is the way to the Father. Along the path, we will learn many of the same lessons, though they will be wrapped in adventures uniquely our own.

In the following pages, I share snippets and insights from my personal walk with Jesus. Though they will be different from yours, the lessons will help you, I hope, when you come to the same point in your walk with Him.

These things I know to be true because I have experienced them: God loves me; He loves you, too. He is faithful; He hears us when we pray; He calls us to be His own. The Lord is full of grace. He has a plan for each of us. He heals; He provides; He protects. He disciplines those He loves. He has a sense of humor. He has a job for us to do—to love Him first and to love others as ourselves.

He has called us to a life filled with faith, hope and love. The greatest of these is love.

A visitor to our home declared once that amazing things happened in my life because I was a mystic. Trust me, I am no mystic! I am an extremely ordinary woman who loves a God who does extraordinary things—every day!

My hope in writing this book is not that you will look at me or at my life, but that through my experiences, you will learn to look into your own life and see God.

Enjoy the journey,

Sue

FAITH

"We live by faith, not by sight."
2 Corinthians 5:7

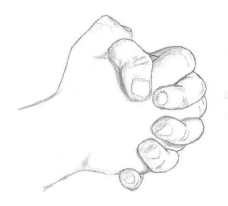

THE TREE OF LIFE

It only seems appropriate that I would begin writing this book while lying in bed recovering from surgery to remove warts from the bottom of my feet. That is what this book is all about—God's incredible love for me, for us—warts and all. It's about His redeeming love. It's about life's messes and His grace.

I, along with many others in my church, am reading through the Bible in a year. Yesterday, the day of my surgery, found me in Leviticus (not exactly the "pick-me-upper" I was looking for!) It said, "Do not offer to the LORD the blind, the injured or the maimed, or anything with *warts* or festering or running sores" (Leviticus 22:22, emphasis added). Though He was talking about animal sacrifices, I took it personally. But this morning, the Lord reminded me of "The Tree."

There is a tree in my old neighborhood that is perfect. It is the most beautiful tree I have ever seen. One cold, dreary winter day, I was, shall we say, in a bad mood. I was angry with my husband, angry with my kids and angry at the world. I was miserable and not very pleasant to be around. I jumped into the car headed for nowhere, but it didn't help because I had come with me. I was crying until I came to "The Tree." I immediately broke out in a smile and was flooded with peace. I pulled over and said, "Lord, why does that tree make me so happy? Look at it; it's nothing but an empty, dry, dead tree!"

I heard Him say to my heart, "What do you see when you look at this tree?" I replied, with a softened heart, "I see it as it is for two weeks in the autumn. I see it full, with bright orange and pink leaves catching the sunlight and shining like a beacon. I see it perfect, in all of its glory."

The Lord said, "That's how I see you. You may feel empty, dry and dead, but I see you through the blood of My Son. I see you full, perfect, in all of your glory."

And that's the truth of who we are in Christ.

I had reconnected with the Creator who makes all things beautiful in their time—even me. Leviticus was the old; Jesus is the new. My hope is not in my perfection but in His grace. We are indeed new creations in Christ. That is why I can share my failures: they are always followed by His work in my life.

That, too, is what this book is all about. It's full of life's lessons; true stories from adventures with my Father, the Almighty. It's about seeing God in the everyday. It comes from time spent with Him—talking to Him, hearing from Him, learning how to walk the path, warts and all. It's about falling in love with Jesus.

THE CROWN

My life goals were crystal clear by the age of eight: I wanted to have a lot of boyfriends, become Miss America and lay down my crown before the end of my reign to join the convent.

By the time I was in the eighth grade, my goal had been refined: I just wanted to become a nun. That summer I went to the Mother House in Pennsylvania and met with the Mother Superior. My desire was to become a novice while attending high school and then take my final vows after graduation. With wisdom that could only have come from God, she told me that she didn't believe I was called to be a nun. She felt that I devoutly admired a particular nun and wanted to be just like her.

She was right. Sister Florence Regina was everything I wanted to be. She was young, beautiful and unashamed of her love for Jesus. When I asked her why she never married, she said, "I am—to Jesus!" Right then and there, I decided I could never do better than that. I wanted Jesus, too. But Mother Superior sent me home to wait and see what God had planned for my life.

Two weeks later I met my one true love, Loren. We were thirteen when we met, fourteen when we started dating and nineteen when we got married. On the day we met with our parish priest to prepare for the wedding, he told us that my father would not be allowed to give me away because my parents were going through a divorce. The priest believed it would be a mockery for my father to participate.

He was still my father, however, and with my mother's blessing, I wanted him to walk me down the aisle and give my hand to Loren in marriage. When the priest refused, I went to a different Catholic church and received permission to have the wedding of my dreams.

Week after week in the months preceding our wedding, I sat under the teaching of my parish priest with whom I was so angry. In fact, I grew to hate him. After Loren and I were married, I stopped attending church altogether.

It took me nine years to realize the pitiful state I was in. I had a wonderful husband, two great kids and a beautiful home, yet I was miserable. Something was missing in my life. I decided it was time to go back to church.

I found a new church with a new priest who had no connection to my past. There God met me the only way I would recognize Him: He met me in Communion. As a Catholic, I knew I couldn't receive Communion because I hadn't been to church or confession in nine years. As I watched with tear-filled eyes as others went forward to receive, I felt that I needed Him more than anyone else in that room. I begged God to let me come; and somehow, in my heart, I knew it was okay. He wanted me, too.*

Two weeks later, I found the courage to go to confession. When I told the priest it had been nine years since my last confession, he asked me why. I was shocked! He wasn't supposed to talk to me—just listen to my confession, give me penance and absolution and send me on my way.

I proceeded to tell him the story of the priest and his refusal to allow my father to be a part of our wedding.

"He was wrong," he said.

Yes, I knew it! I thought triumphantly.

Then he broke my silent victory. "But you were more wrong than he was. You held God and an entire church responsible for the actions of one man. You are forgiven, but you need to go do business with God."

I knelt in the pew and prayed with all my heart. I asked God to forgive me and I forgave the priest.

At that moment, with eyes closed, I saw a cave with a huge stone in front of it. As I spoke the words of forgiveness, the stone rolled away and a brilliant light poured out. I was forgiven and Jesus' death was not in vain in my life.

I believe the door to the Kingdom of God was unlocked for me that day. And years later, at the funeral of a dear friend, there was a beautiful reconciliation between my family and the priest of my youth. God had spoken to his heart and, in humility, he asked for forgiveness. God's healing was complete—for all of us.

Even though I am no longer a member of the Catholic Church, I am forever grateful for the foundation of faith that was birthed in me there.

I eventually made my way back to the convent where I had spent much of my childhood helping the nuns. As I stood facing the convent, I wondered if I had missed God's calling. But immediately He filled my heart with peace. He showed me that, as a child, I truly wanted to serve Him. In my limited understanding, I thought that meant that, if you were a man, you became a priest; and if you were a woman, you became a nun. He assured me that I had fulfilled my call to serve Him as a wife, mother and teacher of His truth.

At the age of 28, my life's goal not only became crystal clear again, but it became a reality. He gave me nothing I asked for and everything I desired. I have received my crown—a crown of righteousness that I will one day lay at the feet of Jesus. I belong to Him. I am the Bride of Christ. And you really can't do better than that!

*2 Chronicles 30:18–20: "Although most of the many people who came ... had not purified themselves, yet they ate the Passover, contrary to what was written. But Hezekiah prayed for them saying, 'May the LORD, who is good, pardon everyone who sets his heart on seeking God—the LORD, the God of his fathers—even if he is not clean according to the rules of the sanctuary.' And the LORD heard Hezekiah and healed the people."

FREEDOM

My sister Diane had invited us to her home for a Fourth of July picnic. The year was 1981 and it really was a Norman Rockwell kind of day. The street was closed as the children had a bike parade with red, white and blue crepe paper decorating their spokes. The weather was perfect and everyone was having a good time. We felt like the all-American family. Let freedom ring!

I was at the side of the house playing horseshoes. It was my turn. I swung back in "perfect form" when Keith, our six-year-old son, walked right behind me. He caught the brunt of a metal horseshoe in full swing against his face. We were both crying as I carried him into the house. His face was grossly swollen and already turning black and blue.

Diane thought quickly of her next-door neighbor, who was an EMT. Jeff came immediately to help. He looked at Keith, who was lying on the sofa, and said that he was fortunate in that the horseshoe had caught him between the jaw and cheekbone. Nothing was broken.

I thanked Jeff profusely as Keith and I walked him to the door. Then he stopped suddenly and asked, "Would you mind if I prayed for Keith?"

Of course I didn't mind; I was grateful. He knelt beside Keith at the threshold of the front door and laid his hand on my son's face and prayed. He prayed as I had never heard before. He prayed as if he was actually speaking to God Himself; and he waited and listened as if God was answering him. Then he smiled and handed my son back to me, assuring me that Keith was healed.

Keith kept saying over and over that Jesus had healed him. And a mere fifteen minutes later, as we were all sitting around the table, I glanced over and was in awe of the sight before my eyes. There was Keith, laughing, eating and totally healed. There was no swelling or bruising – only a small blue dot at the point of impact. And he said he had no pain. I went over and held him, thanking God for the miracle He had performed for our son.

I also knew it was a miracle in how He had spoken to Jeff. Suddenly I was faced with the reality of God—not as a religion, but as a living and active Creator who cares about everything that touches our lives. This revelation simmered on the burner of my soul.

Months later I was still thinking about the day God had healed our son. It was during this time that I started going back to church—when I discovered that something was missing in my life. Peace was far from me. I was actually full of fear. It had such a grip on me that many times I felt as if I couldn't breathe. I was afraid to be alone. Few knew how badly I was suffering. I was too ashamed to tell them.

Then the thought came to me: *Call Jeff.* I called my sister to get his number, but Jeff answered the phone instead. Diane wasn't home; he just happened to be thawing hamburger in her microwave. We had a divine phone appointment that day. I poured my fears out to him and he listened with ears in tune with the wisdom of God.

He comforted me with truth from the Bible, which he said was God's Word. He explained that a battle was raging for my soul but that the devil was a liar. He told me Jesus had promised that His sheep would hear His voice and follow Him. I was being called to follow. And then Jeff extended the most gracious gift—he offered to teach me from the Scriptures and the things of God's Spirit.

With my husband's approval, Jeff came every Friday and opened my eyes and heart to the truth. I couldn't wait for Fridays to come because God came on Fridays. I didn't think Jeff *was* God; I just knew that he brought God with him. It was the most glorious time. I was changing.

There was not a single defining moment when fear left me; it was just gone. It had been replaced with the peace of God in my heart and mind.

One night as I lay in bed, I got to thinking. I didn't want God to come only on Fridays! I wanted Him on Wednesdays and on Mondays. In fact, I wanted Jesus all the time, and I wanted all He had for me. Right then and there, I gave my life to Christ and He filled me with His Holy Spirit.

Three months passed, and Loren came home early one day to sit in on Jeff's teaching. I had said, "But Jeff said—" so often I think Loren wanted to prove that Jeff didn't know everything. He threw some trick questions Jeff's way. Undisturbed, Jeff ignored what he was asking and continued on a completely different topic. I felt sorry for Loren. Jeff didn't seem to be listening to him at all.

But what confused me even more was Loren's reaction. He would ask another question and then sit back, amazed at the answer that didn't make any sense. At the end of the evening, I discovered that Jeff didn't answer any of Loren's trick questions because God was answering the real questions unspoken in Loren's heart.

God had captured our souls, and three weeks later, while driving home from work, alone in his truck, Loren gave his life to the Lord.

It all began on that beautiful Fourth of July in 1981. It was an ordinary day filled with family, games, hot dogs and watermelon. And then an extraordinary thing happened: God's healing grace appeared at the threshold and changed our lives forever. So, let freedom ring indeed! Freedom from the lies of the devil; freedom from the penalty of sin; freedom from fear; and, for those who say, "Yes, Lord," the freedom to become the children of God.

THE BLUE BLANKET

One night, many years ago, I had one of those rare, leisurely moments for the mother of two small children. I was soaking in a warm bath and enjoying the quiet. Suddenly my thoughts (or lack thereof!) were interrupted by a picture that flashed through my mind. I saw a row of ten small shacks. The third house in had its porch light on and somehow I knew I was supposed to take a blue wool blanket to an old man there on Thursday night.

I wasn't sure what this all meant, but it seemed so real. My husband assured me that God was speaking to me in a vision.

I had several days to wrestle with the idea. I was determined to go, but maybe I should take the brown blanket (it was bigger) or the electric blanket (it was warmer). Why do we try to improve on God's plan? In the end, I took the blue wool blanket.

On Thursday night I dressed up, and Loren and I, along with our children, Keith and Cheryl, and our friend Jeff piled into the car, when we suddenly realized we had no idea where we were going. I just said, "Go that way, and if it's the Lord, He'll lead us." We drove for several miles and there, on the left-hand side of the road, was a row of ten small shacks, and the third one in had its porch light on, exactly as I had seen.

I grabbed the blanket as Loren and I got out of the car. It was a terrible, frightening place, and I was afraid. So I knelt down right there on the gravel path and prayed, "Lord, are You sure this is where I'm supposed to be?" And in my heart I heard, "Don't be afraid; I am with you."

Loren and I went and knocked on the door. There I was in my Sunday best, clutching the blue blanket, when an angry, grungy man with no shirt, belt buckle open, tattoos everywhere, and long, dirty hair opened the door. I swallowed hard and managed to say, "Um, excuse me. God told me to give you this blanket."

Looking shocked, he said, "*What?*"

So I said again, "God told me to give you this blanket."

With as much contempt as he could muster, he snarled, "Let me get this straight. God came out of heaven, sat on your couch and told you to give me this blanket?"

"No," I answered, "but He told me to come to *this* house with *this* blanket on *this* night!"

He opened the door wider and said, with an evil grin and intimidating voice, "Well, come on in and we'll talk about it."

When he opened the door, I could see the entire house. It was only one room. I saw a mattress on the floor, a rickety dining room chair and what looked like a camp stove. It was knee-deep in dirty clothes, with beer and liquor bottles and pornography everywhere.

But for some reason, I was no longer afraid. I stated firmly that I would not come in, and that I was there only to give him the blanket.

He started yelling, "Lady, you're freaking me out! Get out of here! I don't want you, I don't want your God and I don't want that blanket! Now get out!"

I turned to leave, but turned back again. "I know God said to come," I pleaded. "He specifically said tonight, Thursday, with this blue wool blanket."

Just then, another man stepped out from behind the door. He had tears in his eyes and said quietly, "It's mine. I'll take it. I'll take anything you have for me."

In some way I couldn't explain, I recognized him, though I had never seen him before in my life. I handed him the blanket and smiled.

"Did a church send you?" he asked.

"No, God sent me, and He wants you to know that He loves you very much."

He returned a shy smile and said, "I know He does. Thank you for coming."

Loren and I walked back to the car. As we drove off, we could still hear the first man screaming, "You're freaking me out! You're freaking me out!"

Back in the car, Jeff, Keith and Cheryl told us they had been praying and singing to the Lord. Loren had stood by me, never saying a word, but praying the whole time.

Three evenings later, I was quietly reliving the adventure in my mind. I could think of little else. Loren and I had been taught that whenever God uses you to bless another person, it's always for you first. He could have sent anyone, but He chose to send me because I had something to learn. What was He trying to teach me?

Suddenly it hit me. Something was wrong. I went to the Lord in prayer.

"Father, You said I would see an old man there. Both of those guys were younger than I am."

"There was an old man there," He assured me.

"No, Lord," I said, "they were both younger."

"There was an old man there."

"Lord, they were younger! Was there someone else hiding behind the door?"

It was then that the Spirit of God spoke to my heart. "*You were the old man.*"

I gasped and cried, "No, Lord! I never lived like that! I was a good person. When I was young, I didn't drink or do drugs. I never had sex before I was married. For goodness' sake, I was going to be a nun!"

But God opened my eyes to see that, before I let the blood of Jesus cleanse me, my "house" was as filthy as theirs. Sin is sin. The only difference between them and me was Jesus. In my pride and ignorance, I could see why those men needed Jesus, but I was already good—and, basically, God was lucky to have me on His team. The Lord showed me that love (the blue blanket) covers a multitude of sin. For the first time, I understood the meaning of grace.

I closed my eyes and saw the man and his filthy house and I opened my heart to see Isaiah 64:6: "All of us have become like one who is unclean, and all our righteous acts are like filthy rags."

I didn't feel condemned; I felt loved. That night I understood who I really was and what God had done for me through Jesus. I had no right to judge other people. God loves us all and desires that none should perish. God, I discovered, is the Captain, and no one is so bad that He doesn't want them or so good that they deserve to be on His team. He loves us all and has made a way for us to be with Him forever.

Romans 5:8 says, "But God demonstrates his own love for us in this: While we were still sinners, Christ died for us." God's grace is undeserved and flowing.

BLIND FAITH

I started taking ballet lessons when I was six years old. And although I took them for only one year, they left a lasting impression on my life. So when our daughter, Cheryl, turned six, we gave her dance lessons for her birthday. She hated them. She loved ballet, but the class was chaotic and she would always come out crying. I decided to call my former ballet teacher to see what she would recommend for Cheryl.

Madame Binda was thrilled to hear from me after almost thirty years and said she would love to take Cheryl as her student. I couldn't believe she was still teaching after all those years.

When we arrived for the first class, it was a flashback. She looked exactly the same—a little older, perhaps, but still beautiful and graceful. The studio hadn't changed either. It was in the basement of her house, with mirrors and barres all around and a black and white checkered dance floor. She was a wonderful teacher, loving yet firm, and Cheryl loved her and the girls in her class right away.

In the middle of that first dance class, Madame Binda stopped the music and turned to me and said, "I do remember you. You had trouble with fifth position and were always talking to Diane Abels." One year almost thirty years ago and she still remembered!

Cheryl danced under her direction for five years while, at the same time, using her gift to glorify God with our worship dance group at church.

But this story isn't about dancing. It's about what happened during the last year of our time with Madame Binda. She had an elderly aunt living with her who was very sick. She was frail, would quietly speak in French while shuffling slowly down the hall to her room and always stayed upstairs, on the main floor where her bedroom was located.

One day Madame Binda asked me to make a cup of tea for her aunt. As I was walking up the stairs from the basement studio, I felt a strong urge from the Holy Spirit to share the gospel with her. I tried to make the urge go away. I argued with the Lord all the reasons I couldn't do it. For one thing, she was from Belgium and couldn't speak English and I couldn't speak French. I thought that was perhaps a significant point He hadn't considered.

The truth was, I was afraid of what Madame Binda would think. We can be so selfish sometimes.

I brought the tea that day but didn't share with her the hope I had found in Jesus. I failed.

The next week I took Cheryl to ballet class and Madame Binda asked the girls to pray for her aunt, who was in the hospital and not expected to live. Fear and shame strangled me. I had not been obedient to share the gift of salvation with a dying woman. I begged the Lord to give me a second chance. And I begged Him not to let her die until someone gave her His message of love.

The next week we arrived at class and Madame Binda asked me to take tea to her aunt upstairs. She was home from the hospital. I was filled with gratitude, as well as shame, as I realized that I still didn't want to do it. Heart pounding, I dragged myself up those stairs knowing that God had given me a second chance. I wouldn't fail again.

I made the tea and walked slowly back to her room. She looked beautiful lying peacefully in her bed. I sat on the edge and she sat up to drink the tea. I reached out my hand and rubbed her back and asked, "Lord, what do You want to say to her?"

"Tell her that I love her and have prepared a place for her."

Unfortunately, at that very moment, I remembered that I couldn't speak French. I tried opening my mouth, thinking that French would just come out—but it didn't! I felt the Lord smile and whisper, "Just tell her."

So I gave her His message of love. She looked up and tilted her head to one side.

"Do you know Jesus?" I asked. "Do you know how much He loves you? Do you know that He paid the price for your sins when He died on the cross for you and for me? Do you know that He rose from the dead and has prepared a place for you where you can be with Him forever? Do you want to ask Jesus into your heart and, when you leave here, go and be with Him? He's waiting for you."

She took my hands in hers and whispered, "Jesus." I prayed for her and kissed her on her forehead. She looked my way and said (in English!), "Who are you? I can't see you. I can only see your eyes."

I told her that my name was Sue Nystrom and that I had taken ballet lessons from Madame Binda many years ago and now my daughter was in her class. We sat holding hands for a few minutes. Then she said again, "Who are you? I can't see you. I can only see your eyes."

28

I told her the same thing again, but before I could finish, she said, "Who are you? I can't see you. I can only see your eyes."

This time I was silent, kissed her forehead again and said, "Jesus loves you so much," and left.

She died the following week. After the funeral, Madame Binda came up to me and asked what had happened that last day I had been in her aunt's room. It was the very question I dreaded. I faced our dear teacher and told her that I had given her aunt a message from God about His love for her. Then I added, "It was strange, though. Three times she asked me, 'Who are you? I can't see you. I can only see your eyes.'"

Madame Binda's eyes filled with tears. "My aunt has been totally blind for three years," she said.

It was then that I understood. Her aunt had not been seeing me at all. She had been looking into the eyes of Jesus and He was welcoming her home.

A SPIRITUAL GIFT

She was in her eighth month of pregnancy and had been bedridden most of that time. It had been a long ordeal and my friend was feeling depressed and discouraged. I went over to spend some time with her and help set up the nursery. It was beautiful.

Her family had pitched in to help with the cooking and cleaning during those long months. They did a good job except in one area. The kitchen floor hadn't been scrubbed in months. As you can imagine, it was filthy.

Because she had a doctor's appointment that afternoon, I asked if I could stay and scrub her floor. She was grateful. Minutes before her departure, she received a phone call from another friend of ours. This woman had a prophecy about the baby, and my friend's countenance changed completely. She was light and happy again, and walked out the door a new woman.

I walked into the kitchen a changed woman, too.

I was angry and pouting. Since I had been with her all day, the Lord could have used me to speak His words of hope and encouragement. That was spiritual. Instead, I was scrubbing the kitchen floor. Anyone could scrub a floor.

His gentle Spirit spoke to mine, "Anyone *could* scrub a kitchen floor, but not everyone *would*. Are you willing to serve Me the way I choose?"

I needed a life lesson in humility. I got down on my hands and knees and began to scrub—back and forth, back and forth, with a lot of effort and elbow grease. Then I noticed the pattern in the floor and discovered that if I followed the pattern set before me, it took half the energy with twice the results. *Hmmm.* What was the Lord trying to show me? When I do things my own way, in my own strength, it's twice as hard and the results are poor. But when I follow His pattern, His instructions, I can accomplish so much more. His way is always better. Romans 12:2 says, "Do not conform any longer to the pattern of this world, but be transformed by the renewing of your mind. Then you will be able to test and approve what God's will is—his good, pleasing and perfect will."

I thanked God for choosing me to scrub the floor. Apparently I had a lot to learn. By now I was humming. The work went much more quickly with my new attitude and insight. I reached the last square tile—and then I stopped.

There lying in front of me was a great temptation. If I scrubbed this last tile, no one would know how dirty it had been or how much work I had done. And if I didn't scrub it, they would see the contrast between how dirty the floor had been and how clean it was now. It was a ridiculous thought that I entertained ever so briefly. I wouldn't dare let it pass my lips (though I'm writing it in a book!), but God knows our thoughts before we even speak them. It was time for a serious conversation.

"Look at the floor," He said. "Is it clean?"

"No," I replied, "not completely."

"Then not at all. And so it is with sin. You can't hide a

'little' sin in your heart and think you are clean. I didn't come to make you almost clean. I died to make you clean. I finished the job; now finish yours."

I confessed the sin God knew was hidden in my heart for some time. As I scrubbed the last tile, I realized the foolishness of holding onto sin in order to impress others with how clean I am now compared to what I had been. After I repented, this Scripture blazed in my soul: "'Come now, let us reason together,' says the LORD. 'Though your sins are like scarlet, they shall be as white as snow'" (Isaiah 1:18).

When Jesus was dying on the cross, He said, "It is finished." In that instant, He made a way for a heart like mine to be clean, truly clean.

Through the gift of repentance and His death on the cross, my heart is made white as snow—white as that "new" kitchen floor.

Scrubbing a floor can be very spiritual.

THE GREAT RIDDLE

Loren came home from work all excited one day. He had a question burning in his heart to ask me: "Which came first, the chicken or the egg?"

Can you feel the disappointment?

"The chicken," I said.

"Nope!" he said with a mischievous grin.

So I said, "The egg."

He actually laughed out loud. "No." Then he proceeded to tell me that God had given him the answer to this ancient riddle in the book of Genesis. He grabbed his Bible and read aloud: "Then God said, 'Let the land produce vegetation: seed-bearing plants and trees on the land that bear fruit *with seed in it*, according to their various kinds" (Genesis 1:11, emphasis added). He went on to read that "God made ... all the creatures that move along the ground according to their kinds" (verse 25).

"Don't you see?" exclaimed Loren. "They came together! God created the chicken with the egg in it!"

It was pretty neat, I had to admit, but I wondered why God would waste a revelation on a riddle.

I found my answer the following weekend in the Sunday

paper. It was the first Sunday that a new feature would be running in the magazine section of the newspaper. A woman claiming the highest IQ in the nation would answer questions week by week sent in to her by readers. Guess what the first question was: "Which came first, the chicken or the egg?"

I honestly can't remember what her answer was, but she gave a scientific reason for one or the other. Then it struck me: One revelation from God is greater than all the wisdom of the world.

Now I was as excited as Loren had been. I started praying for this woman regularly, and followed her column with great interest. She really was brilliant—which is why I was so surprised at her answer four weeks later to this question: "If you were stranded on a desert island, which four books would you take with you?" She said she would take a dictionary, a thesaurus, *Uncle Ben's Quote Book* and a New York telephone directory.

Can you feel the disappointment?

I could stand it no longer. I went to the store and bought a Bible and had her name engraved on it. I sat down and wrote her a letter explaining the chicken and the egg. I then expressed my hope that if she were ever stranded anywhere, she would take her Bible along with her since it held all the wisdom she would ever need. I took the package to the post office and sent it on its way with a prayer.

And then I panicked. I worried for the next three days that I would be investigated as a fanatic and put on a list of possible stalkers. Like a scene from the television show *Laverne & Shirley*, I dreamed up ways to sneak into her office and intercept the package before she opened it.

On the third day after mailing the letter and Bible, I arrived at work (I was the librarian at a small Christian school

34

at the time) and went straight to my desk. I couldn't believe my eyes. Sitting there in a neat stack were four books: a dictionary, a thesaurus, a copy of *Uncle Ben's Quote Book* (which I didn't even know we owned) and, sitting right on top, the Holy Bible. I knew God was confirming that the columnist had indeed been delivered His personal message of wisdom. It was now in His hands.

I never heard from her, but I knew I was simply called to give her His message. The rest is between them.

I believe with all my heart that God Himself will reveal to her what He has revealed to us in Psalm 111:10: "The fear of the LORD is the beginning of wisdom; all who follow his precepts have good understanding. To him belongs eternal praise."

FOLLOW THAT TRUCK!

In the early days of my walk with the Lord, I belonged to a women's Bible study that met at our church. This group, "Daily Bread," was a powerful source of nourishment for my soul. Each Wednesday we would pray, worship, study, have group discussion and fellowship. I grew in the strength and knowledge of the Lord through the leadership of godly women I still love and admire to this day.

Our children, meanwhile, learned to offer their gifts and talents to the Lord at an early age with the encouragement of these dear ones. Keith was invited to sing songs of praise several times—the lone boy standing courageously before a group of women. He and Cheryl led the group once in singing Christmas carols. And when Cheryl was only seven years old, she choreographed and performed a beautiful dance to the carol, "What Child Is This?" by hymn writer William Dix. Her dance represented the struggle in Mary's heart as she held her precious infant ever so briefly, knowing all along that she would have to let Him go. Yes, she was a mother holding her son, but He was her Savior as well.

At the close of each week, we would pass around a basket filled with slips of paper containing prayer requests people had phoned into the church office. We didn't know most of the people we were praying for, but we made a commitment to hold them in prayer every day for one week.

I received a request for a young man who had been in a horrific motorcycle accident and wasn't expected to live through the night. The person making the request was crying out for healing and salvation for this one in such desperate need of a miracle from God. I fervently asked God for those very things.

To my surprise, the following Wednesday, as God would have it, the prayer request I drew from the basket was for the same young man. He had made it through the week in a coma and was still in need of healing and salvation.

Once again the next week, I received a request for Stephen (I now knew his name), who was out of the coma but still in critical condition requiring surgery.

From that point on, the leaders just handed me any requests or updates that came in for Stephen, as the Lord had somehow knit my heart to his. I continued to pray for his healing and salvation every day for the next three months.

Gradually I began receiving praise reports: Stephen's surgeries were successful. Stephen accepted the Lord. Stephen was reading his Bible. Stephen was released from the hospital. The last slip of paper I received on behalf of this young man read, "It's a miracle! Stephen is finally home. He bought a new truck and the license plate says, 'Me & JC' (Jesus Christ). Thank you for your faithfulness in prayer."

Fast forward fifteen years. Loren and I were out for a leisurely Sunday drive through the rolling hills of West Virginia. We were off the beaten path on a beautiful fall day and the scenery was spectacular. Suddenly a red truck appeared on the road in front of us with the license plate that read, *Me &*

JC. As if out of a scene from an action movie, I pointed my finger and shouted, *"Follow that truck!"* My husband, a very good sport, took off after him.

It wasn't exactly a high-speed chase, but it was a wild adventure in the Kingdom of God. Loren did his best not to lose him by staying close and not letting other cars separate us. For ten minutes I chanted, "I can't remember his name. I can't remember his name."

After what seemed like an eternity, we came to a red light. I jumped out of the car, then poked my head back in and exclaimed to Loren excitedly, "It's Stephen! His name is Stephen!" Then I ran ahead to the driver's side of the truck in front of us and tapped on the window. The driver cautiously rolled it down halfway, looking confused. The woman with him didn't look too thrilled either.

"Excuse me," I said, "but is your name Stephen?"

"Yes."

"Well, you don't know me, but fifteen years ago you were in a motorcycle accident and I prayed for you."

Suddenly the light turned green. That was it. I smiled and waved and said, "Okay, well, God bless you!" They drove off and I ran back to the car and jumped in.

My knees were knocking and my hands were trembling as I buckled my seatbelt. Amazed and breathless, I whispered, "What on earth was that all about?"

Loren said wisely, "He must be struggling with his faith. He just needed to know that the God who loved him then loves him now." God never gives up on us.

James 5:15 says, "And the prayer offered in faith will make the sick person well; the Lord will raise him up." I, along with many others, prayed for Stephen's healing and salvation. Jesus raised him up with a plan and purpose for his life. He isn't going to lose him. The Lord is faithful and will complete the good work He has begun.

I had the privilege of holding Stephen in the arms of prayer through the infancy of his faith. Jesus healed and restored him, and the Holy Spirit will continue to provide the daily bread of faith and encouragement needed to give him (and all of us) the strength to finish the journey.

GET REAL

I know you're not allowed to have favorites, but if I did, Don would have to be right up there on top. Of all the people who have ever lived with us, he was the most fun.

We met Don at a Bible study while he was still in college. He started spending the night with us on Tuesdays. The kids loved him. He and Keith made great forts out of furniture and he taught Cheryl how to ride her two-wheeler. They would make up silly songs together. My favorite was "Chomping on Socks," which came with props—a drawer full of socks that would go flying into the air at just the right moment. Their love for singing together grew. Many years later, Don asked Cheryl to sing with him on his worship CD. They have sung together since she was four, and you can hear it in their familiar harmonies.

I used to love Wednesdays. Loren and I never set the alarm on Tuesday nights, but we always woke up early Wednesday morning in joyful anticipation. Don would greet us behind the closed door with an original little ditty he would sing, or creatively impersonate "The Professor" who would, for example, inform us of everything there was to know about the monarch butterfly. Needless to say, life was never dull with

Don around.

After he graduated from college, Don needed a place to live, and we jumped at the opportunity to have him join our family. He lived with us for six months. During that time, in Don's eyes, Loren and I quickly fell off our pedestals; and we discovered that he wasn't perfect either. It was great. It was real! We discovered, for instance, that Don had a habit of writing notes to himself. That's okay. I do, too. Unfortunately, he did it on little sticky notes plastered all over the house—the bathroom mirror, the front door, the kids' bedroom doors—everywhere. I finally put my foot down: all notes were to be contained within the confines of his own bedroom.

If you must know, I had a little habit of my own. When baking cakes, I used canned chocolate icing and always saved a little in the bottom of the can. Later, I could scoop my finger in and eat it by itself. So it came as a great surprise when I opened the can one day, stuck in my finger and pulled out a note that read, "Gotcha!" I called Don at work and said, "I can't believe you put a note in my icing!" He shot back, "I can't believe you already found it and it's only ten in the morning!"

That was life with Don. He wasn't only fun. He, more than anyone I knew, had an intense passion for Jesus. He was a man after God's own heart. We learned a lot from each other during that time.

At one point, however, I developed a severe case of "super-spirituality." Everything was intense, everything was dramatic, and everything had a deeper meaning. I was tough to be around.

One day when I went to visit my friend Maria, she wondered at my lack of joy. We prayed together, and she envisioned Jesus and me walking on the beach holding hands, just talking. As she shared it, I clearly saw it, too. Then it

41

happened—Jesus bent down and splashed me! Maria and I saw it at the exact same moment. She started laughing, but I became even more serious. Obviously it was a symbol of baptism, of cleansing from some horrible sin. Maria looked at me with disbelief. Then she spoke these words directly from the heart of God: "Lighten up!"

Later that night, Loren, Don and I were discussing our day and what the Lord had taught us. I shared my story. The next morning, I awoke to Don serenading me with this song:

> *Morning shines its light through your window*
> *Its rays are growing bright and strong*
> *But through the night*
> *There was another Light*
> *Warming you.*
>
> *And He's not like the moon to vanish*
> *When first comes the light of day*
> *And He's here now to greet you*
> *To say, "Good morning, it's a brand-new day.*
> *Come on, let's play. Come on, let's play."*

The heaviness lifted and the joy of the Lord was again my strength. God laughs.

But there are other times in our walk with Christ when things aren't so fun—times we have important life lessons to learn. We rarely choose them; they find us. Such it was one night when Don asked if some friends could stay with us for the weekend in order to attend the wedding for a friend of theirs from college.

Loren and Keith had left for Ecuador on a three-week mission trip and I was alone with Cheryl. I thought it would be fun to have a house full of people. It turned out to be wall-to-wall fun.

Don's friends arrived the day before the wedding, bringing with them a man Don had never met. They all decided to go out that night—with the exception of this one individual, who said he wasn't feeling well. They left, and I didn't think anything about it, until the man came out of his room and said, "Did you know I used to be a man of violence?" Then he disappeared into his room again.

Why I didn't take Cheryl and leave the house, I'll never know. The thought just never crossed my mind. Instead, I called my neighbor and asked her to come over and stay with us that evening. We prayed together, and while she was there, I had peace. She left close to midnight and I went downstairs and put Cheryl into bed with me. Then, like any mature adult, I pulled the covers over my head, thinking no evil could find us there.

The man never came out of his room, but I could hear him pacing the floor while I shook with fear. As I prayed, I heard an almost audible voice saying, "Don't be afraid, I am with you."

I knew He was with me, but I begged Jesus to make Don come home.

Minutes later I heard once again, "Don't be afraid, I am with you."

I said again that I knew, but I begged Him to make Loren come home (from Ecuador, that very moment!).

As I continued in my fear, I heard those precious words a third time, "Don't be afraid, I am with you."

"I know!" I shouted back. *"But I want someone who's real!"*

I couldn't believe those words had come out of my mouth.

Not in anger, but in pure compassion, the Lord said, "No one is more real than I am. I am your protector. I am your comfort. I am your peace. I am with you. Don't be afraid."

Fear fled. Total peace filled the room. Cheryl and I were safe in the watchful care of Jesus.

If you had asked me before that night if I believed God is real, I would have answered with an emphatic yes. But I had foolishly sought the protection of what I could see and had denied the power of our unseen God. I was sad to discover such doubt hiding deep within my heart. But my Father didn't leave me sad or fearful or confused. He promises to contend with those who contend with me. He calls me the apple of His eye. I had no reason to doubt Him. I needed to be aware of the unbelief in my heart so it could be converted to faith. Like the father of the deaf and mute son in Mark 9:24, I could exclaim, "I do believe; help me overcome my unbelief!"

Don hates this story. It hurts his heart to think that he had somehow put us in danger. He felt responsible to keep us safe. That's what love does: it always protects. But no matter how much we long for that to be true, the reality is that we can't always be there for each other. Only God is able. He promises never to leave us or forsake us. He means that literally—He is always with us. Psalm 4:8 says, "I will lie down and sleep in peace, for you alone, O LORD, make me dwell in safety."

He is the Light warming us, protecting us through the night, waiting to greet us with a brand-new day. "This is the day the LORD has made; let us rejoice and be glad in it" (Psalm 118:24). God laughs, not at us but with us in victory. He sees us through whatever trials may come and then invites us with joy as He calls out to us, "Come on, let's play."

PERSONAL PRAYER

God desires a personal relationship with us, and, like any good relationship, communication is extremely important. Time spent alone with Him is where we get to know Him better and where we can safely share our deepest needs and desires. It's where we discover His plans and purposes for our lives and where we seek and receive understanding. Prayer is where we connect with the One who created us to be the object of His love.

There are many kinds of prayer and different purposes for prayer, but *personal* prayer is simply a conversation between you and God. It is "simply" an awesome miracle that the God who created heaven and earth wants to talk to us and hear from us. He cares about everything that touches our lives and the world around us. Personal prayer is not selfish; it is necessary.

Prayer is not meant to be a monologue; it is a dialogue. I read somewhere that the polite part of prayer is waiting to hear how God will respond. How many times have I thrown up a quick prayer to Him, grabbed my coat and headed out the door, never really expecting Him to answer me at all?

God speaks to His children. He has given us His written word, the Bible, as a gift to be treasured and obeyed. It is the voice of truth, and He calls us to read it, know it, love it and hide it in our hearts so we can know Him better and know His will for our lives. But He is a creative God who is speaking to us all the time in many different ways if we believe and look for Him in the everyday. Think of Moses and the burning bush. God spoke to him after he turned aside to see why the bush was on fire but not burning up. If we put God in a box and determine that He can only speak in old English, we will miss His precious and powerful voice many times as He attempts to get our attention. God will never contradict what He has written in the Bible; but we shouldn't try to limit Him by our own understanding. He is greater than our greatest thought.

I have never heard the audible voice of God, but I know people who have. He can speak to us in that still, small voice or in power enough to quiet a raging storm. God speaks to my heart in ways that I recognize, and then stretches me to search and know Him more. He uses other people, circumstances and even nature itself, His own creation. Romans 1:19-20 tells us that "what may be known about God is plain to them, because God has made it plain to them. For since the creation of the world God's invisible qualities—his eternal power and divine nature—have been clearly seen, being understood from what has been made, so that men are without excuse."

He speaks to us in dreams, visions and prophetic words. He stirs my heart in the words of a song or in the deep thoughts of a child.

One day our friend Don had cried out to the Lord with something that was troubling him deeply. Our daughter, Cheryl, ran downstairs and said, "Don, look! I can read!" She took his Bible and opened it to a psalm. Because she was a beginner, she pointed with her finger at the words she recognized—just those!—and began to read carefully:

46

"The...of...the...and...is...of...at...and...the."

Don closed his eyes and said, "Amen. Thank You, Lord." As he followed her finger and filled in the blanks with the other words written on the page, he received his answer and heard the distinct voice of God lovingly calm his fears.

God used to speak to my husband through vanity license plates. No kidding! In the early days of Loren's walk with the Lord, before he even owned a Bible, he would ask God a question in the morning and, while driving his van on the way to or from work, would see a license plate with a Scripture verse that read something like *John15, Pslm563*(Psalm 56:3) or *Heb116* (Hebrews 11:6). He would have to wait until he got home to look it up in my Bible. And there, waiting for him, would be the answer to his morning question. After two weeks of this happening every day, he finally stopped at the store and bought his own Bible, which he kept on the passenger seat of his van. He couldn't wait until he got home for the answer.

This went on for months. Then one day Loren asked his morning question, and the license plate he found displayed *Eph714*. He had just finished reading Paul's letter to the Ephesians that morning, so he knew there were only six chapters in that book. When he asked what this meant, the Lord showed him that he had received a counterfeit license plate. "You don't need them anymore," the Lord told him. "You can hear Me now."

The Lord has spoken to my heart and brought comfort many times through the tip of my own pen as I waited expectantly with an open journal. Hear our conversation through just one entry:

"Father, I am tired."

"Daughter, I AM! I am all you need. I am your resting place; I am your strength; I am your refuge and I am with you.

47

Come sit with Me and rest. I am making all things new and I have called you by name and chosen you to be a part of what I am about to do. Stay close and follow My lead. Listen, obey, be in awe and enjoy. Though you are weary now, I will infuse you with refreshment and great joy. I will do all I have promised. Though the journey is not easy, it is wonderful. Trust Me, for I am the lover of your soul, and I have called you friend. I will show you great and marvelous things, and I will use you in My Kingdom work. For now, quietly rest and let Me do a restoring work in you so you will be ready when I call. Come, lay your head on My shoulder, and close your eyes and rest. Enjoy My peace once again. I am always faithful and I love you."

Oh, how I love Jesus! Often in my times of weakness, He answers with a reminder of His strength. He gives me fresh insight into just how great He really is and that I am in good and loving hands.

Sometimes there are no words to express our need or our longing. Sighing is a prayer. Peace is His answer. "Help!" is a prayer. "Here I am" is His answer. There are times when we go to God with urgent needs or life-changing situations that need an answer right away, and it seems that He is silent. Be silent with Him. Wait, believe, hope, pray and continue praying until you have come to the place where you are able to hear what He is trying to say. Ask Him to increase your faith. He knows the depth of your need.

We can't *make* God answer us. We are not to demand, but we don't need to beg, either. In Hebrews 4:16, He invites us to "approach the throne of grace with confidence, so that we may receive mercy and find grace to help us in our time of need."

Sometimes we are not sure if "it was just me" or if we really heard God speaking to us in some way. The more we practice listening, the more we will hear. I once heard a pastor tell the story of when his daughter was learning to walk. She would take a few steps and then fall down. He didn't say, "You stupid child, you're never going to learn to walk!" No, he clapped; he got excited; he grabbed his video camera; he picked her up, dusted her off and encouraged her to do it again. He held her hand so she could steady herself. In a week, she was walking on her own and he was a proud papa.

God is our proud Papa. He encourages us to keep trying. There should be nothing we are afraid to ask God. He's not mad or disappointed; He wants us to grow and will instruct us every step of the way.

When asked, "What are you doing during prayer?" someone close to God once said, "I look at God and He looks at me." It's that intimate; He sees you and He cares. He loves to spend time with His children. We can be sure, when we talk, God listens. Let us show Him that same respect. What an awesome privilege we have been given in the gift of prayer!

HOPE

"Find rest, O my soul, in God alone;
my hope comes from him."
Psalm 62:5

GOD IN THE SUFFERING

Why do bad things happen to good people? I don't know. I don't pretend to be a great theologian or scholar. But I have learned a few things in life.

First of all, bad things do happen, but there are no good people. There are nice people who do good things, but Jesus said, "Why do you ask me about what is good? ... There is only One who is good" (Matthew 19:17). Jesus is good because He is God. We are not. Scripture tells us that "all have sinned and fall short of the glory of God" (Romans 3:23). We are all in need of a Redeemer, and He has come.

Second, I think we underestimate the importance and power of suffering. We never choose to suffer, but none of us will leave this earth without experiencing it. I don't want to suffer, but I know that during those times of trial, I have grown stronger in faith and character. Sometimes we bring the pain on ourselves; sometimes we do not. Sometimes we are rescued from our troubles; sometimes it seems we are not. But I know that God is good all the time. So where is He during our times of suffering?

When Keith was three months old, his baby teeth started coming in. At the same time, he got a severe ear infection and the doctor had to put him on some strong antibiotics. He informed us that, as Keith got older, his baby teeth might become discolored, but there would be no damage to his permanent teeth. When he was three years old, his teeth not only became discolored; they rotted. He had to have two teeth pulled. I felt like the world's worst mother; he thought it was great. He'd stick straws in the holes and say he was a walrus. He was the envy of all the boys at preschool. They called him "Keith with no Teeth." He was famous.

But on Easter morning, our little son came into our bedroom in tears. His face was almost unrecognizable. His front tooth had abscessed and his lips had swollen beyond his nose. We called the emergency line for the dentist, who graciously agreed to meet us at his office in spite of it being a holiday. He took one look at Keith and determined that there was no time to wait for the infection to subside; the tooth had to be pulled right away.

The dentist had me and Loren hold Keith down in the chair. Keith was screaming and I was crying. The dentist was firm. I thought he was downright mean. I begged him to stop hurting our son. He kicked me out of the room. He said I was only making things worse. So I paced the waiting room floor, crying and praying.

Loren was left alone to hold his son down. He said it was the hardest thing he ever had to do as a father. He leaned all his weight on Keith while the dentist yanked the tooth and scraped the infection. At one point, Keith looked up at Loren with the most horrified look that spoke volumes: *How could you do this to me? I thought you loved me.* Loren's heart broke, but he knew that the pain Keith was experiencing now was the only way to healing.

I believe this is a picture of God's heart in the midst of our pain. Where is He in our suffering? Right there with us, holding us, helping us get through whatever it takes to bring true healing. He doesn't wait in another room until it's over; He stays with us through it all. I think it breaks His heart to see His children suffer, but He knows it is for our ultimate good.

Many times in our pain, we lash out at God, thinking He's the one hurting us and being downright mean. We say, "How could You do this to me? I thought You loved me." He does. He loves us enough to help us when we can't help ourselves, to hold us when we would run away, to set us free from the very thing causing us the pain, to see it through to the end. And if we let God have His way with us, the end will not be one of pain and sin and suffering, but one of overwhelming joy. No matter what the circumstances may seem, God is good all the time.

LOOKING UP

Okay, I know it's a stretch to expect sympathy when you're sitting all alone in a hot tub at a mountain resort looking into a beautiful night sky, but that's exactly what I was asking for.

I was tired. Things had been hard—too hard for too long. Finances were tight, and even though God had helped us and provided in miraculous ways, I was tired of the battle. I was losing hope.

That's when a friend called and asked if my daughter and I could come to the resort. She had been there all week and wondered if we could stay with her daughter for the last two nights while she and her husband went off to be alone. I said I would be happy to come. Actually, I was more willing than happy.

Before she left to spend time with her husband, my friend and I spent the afternoon together as we watched the girls giggle and play. It was a nice day, but I must admit that I was basically just going through the motions since my troubles were absorbing me. The mountains were beautiful, but I was numb to the gift I had been given. My mind was simply elsewhere.

That evening Cheryl asked if she and her friend Ruth could go swimming in the indoor pool. I took them and watched as they enjoyed life and each other. That's when I noticed the hot tub on the deck. I could clearly see the girls from outside, so I told them where I would be if they needed me.

I climbed in and started to feel the tension melt away. Alone with my thoughts, I began to cry softly. Then I looked up. There must have been a million stars out that night. Even self-pity couldn't keep my heart from singing praises to God and giving Him thanks for the beauty of His creation.

Isaiah 40:26 says, "Lift your eyes and look to the heavens: Who created all these? He who brings out the starry host one by one, and calls them each by name. Because of his great power and mighty strength, not one of them is missing." It was awesome.

As the wonder of the stars filled me, I cried out, "O Lord, thank You for the stars."

I heard a familiar whisper stir within my heart. "What about the ones you can't see?"

I thought about it for a moment. "Well, there are lots of reasons for that. Some are covered by clouds, and some are just too far away, and my eyes are too weak. But I still believe they are there."

That's when God spoke His promise to me: "So it is with My blessings. They may be covered with clouds of circumstances. They may seem far away and your vision has been too weak. But they are real. You haven't even begun to see all I have in store for you and your family. Do you believe?"

"Yes, Lord, just as I believe in the stars I can't see, so I believe in Your blessings."

Through the years, I have seen His blessings over and over again. And when times of doubt or fear try to creep in, I have only to look up and see His promise shining in the sky, and I believe.

OUR HOME

We lived in the perfect neighborhood. On our street alone, there were 52 kids. Everyone seemed to have a son Keith's age and a daughter Cheryl's age. On any given day, you would find a pile of bicycles in someone's front yard, revealing which house the kids had congregated in that day. We loved our home.

Unfortunately, we had bought the house in a land contract deal. They're illegal now, but the way it worked back then was that the deed was put in our name, while the previous owner (who was a real estate agent) kept it in an escrow account. Our mortgage payment went directly to her instead of a bank. My husband's business had merged recently with another company, which the bank considered a new business, so they denied our request for a loan. We thought this land contract deal was the perfect solution. The drawback was that the previous owner could foreclose at any time for any reason.

Times were tough for Loren's company. We never missed a mortgage payment, but we were late several times. Finally, the previous owner had had enough. One Wednesday in August, we received a certified letter stating that if she did not receive the payment by that Friday, she would begin

58

foreclosure proceedings immediately.

I lifted the letter to God; there was no way we could have the payment that soon. When Loren came home, we prayed. We thanked God for our time in that house and for the things He had done while we were there. If He had some other place for us to go, we would go. But if He wanted us to stay, He would have to do something. (I know I made that sound easy; it wasn't!) We didn't know what else to do.

Then He gave us Philippians 4:19: "And my God will meet all your needs according to his glorious riches in Christ Jesus."

At 8:45 that Friday morning, the doorbell rang. I opened the door to a man I had never seen before. A yellow sports car was parked at the curb. He was holding a white envelope.

"Susan?" he said.

"Yes."

"I have something for you."

I accepted the envelope, thanked him and closed the door. Barely breathing, I went back to the family room and sat silently in the recliner, holding the unopened envelope for the longest time, tears trickling down my face. I was convinced it was an eviction notice. Finally, with little faith or hope, I opened the envelope.

Inside were eight one hundred dollar bills.

Tears flowed faster now. I praised God for His faithfulness even when we were not, and I knew for sure that He had more work for us to do in that house.

We still don't know who gave us the money. It could have been someone God spoke to in prayer or it could have been an angel riding in that yellow sports car. Whoever it was, he was sent by God, who had definitely met our needs.

We paid our mortgage and thought everything was settled.

That's why God's instruction came as a total surprise three months later, when I was standing in the kitchen and washing the dishes.

"Sell the house."

"But Lord, You gave it back to us."

"It's time to sell the house."

"How am I ever going to convince Loren?"

That night, when Loren came home from work, he said there was something he needed to talk to me about. I told him I had something to tell him, too, but that he should go first. So he said that while he was working, the Lord told him that it was time to sell the house.

God is so good!

We called a real estate agent who was a Christian and told him the situation. Loren and I had prayed and felt we should put the house on the market for $110,000. But because our real estate agent was convinced that it would not sell for more than $100,000, we ended up listing it for the lower price. I prayed that many people would come through for the blessing, but the agent said not to expect many because the school year had begun and it was a slow time in the housing market.

At the end of the month, 45 people had looked at our house. According to the agent, that was unheard of; everyone moving to Northern Virginia had come through our home! I thanked God for the blessing, but asked Him why none of them had bought it. I clearly understood His answer, "I told you to sell it for $110,000."

So Loren called our agent and told him we needed to raise the price of the house. It made no sense, but the agent knew God's ways were not always our ways. We went to his house with a letter authorizing the price change.

The next morning he brought a couple through the house.

And that night, as I was praying, the number 102 kept going through my mind.

"102 what?" I asked.

"$102,000. That's how much the house will sell for."

"Then why was it so important to list it for $110,000?"

And my heart immediately understood the only word needed to be spoken: "Obedience."

The next day our agent came by for us to sign a contract for $102,000. We had not known it, but the couple had put a contract on the house right away. They had a son Keith's age and a daughter Cheryl's age. They were the ones God had chosen.

They asked for a delayed settlement date. We gratefully accepted the contract in November knowing they wouldn't be moving in until March, which gave us time to locate a rental house. It was hard. Because of our credit history, no one would rent to us.

The day of the settlement came in March but we still had nowhere to live. Somehow, we still had peace. I honestly believed I would see a car with a bumper sticker that read, "Follow me," and we would follow it up the driveway to our new home. It never appeared.

Loren looked over at me in the passenger seat of the car and asked, "Did you just ask the Lord for a license plate?" He smiled and pointed to the car in front of us with the plate which read *Deut869*. We eagerly looked up Deuteronomy 8:6–9:

"Observe the commands of the LORD your God, walking in his ways and revering him. For the LORD your God is bringing you into a good land ... a land where bread will not be scarce and you will lack nothing."

The Lord's promises are true, but it was midnight and we still had nowhere to go. All of our possessions were in a truck parked in front of our friends' house next door to our former home. What were we supposed to do?

Then a friend's words rang in my ear: "If you ever need anything, give me a call."

Maria was a landscape designer, and she and Loren had worked together on projects over the years. He had recently done some work for Maria and her husband, Jack. During that time, Maria was going through a "dark night of the soul," and God used Loren to remind her of the peace He offers each one of us.

I had met Maria only a month earlier, and we instantly became friends. Now here I was calling her at midnight to see if she had room for the four of us. To this day, I can't believe I called her. Almost our entire family lived in the area, and any one of them would gladly have taken us in. But in that moment, Maria was my first and only thought. Strange!

Feeling sorry for us but not really knowing much about us, she called and checked with her husband, who was out of town, and then graciously took us in. God works in mysterious ways.

Every morning for the week that we stayed with Maria, I woke up crying because we had nowhere to live. And every night I thanked God for where He had brought us and for what He had done during the day. The kids thought we were on a great adventure and had a wonderful time with Maria's children. Keith and John Paul went exploring through the woods and creek while Cheryl and Carrie enjoyed swimming in the pool or feeding the horse that lived next door.

God's provision was abundant; Maria's graciousness was priceless. Our every need was met. One evening I even had the audacity to ask her if our friends could come over for a prayer meeting we regularly held in our home. Just as astonishingly, she agreed—and that night Maria was filled with the Holy Spirit. The gift of intercessory prayer was birthed in her that night. She didn't sleep, but saw a "newsreel" of faces from around the world that ran through her mind as she prayed for each of them throughout the night. She "woke up" refreshed. God knew the plans He had for all of us.

The next morning I was crying again, and Maria comforted me with the promise of hope. God had given her a vision of our new home. It was a beautiful white house with pillars, sitting high on a hill. We had been looking at what we could afford, but God was undaunted by our circumstances. He had a great blessing awaiting us.

After a week, we left Maria's house and went to stay with my sister and her family in their mobile home. Diane took good care of us, and her home became our refuge. The kids loved being with their cousins. Cheryl and Tracy had grown up together more as best friends than cousins, and Keith and Troy had many an escapade in the short time we were together. It was a comfort to have the warmth of family love and understanding. We stayed with them for several days, and then we moved on to the one-bedroom apartment of our friends Jim and Kathy. My sister kindly kept our cats with her the whole time we were wandering. (Honest, Diane, I didn't know Rascal was pregnant!)

During the week we spent at Jim and Kathy's, we enjoyed the sweetest time of fellowship. They kept pointing us to the hope we have in Jesus. It was great being there, but I was getting discouraged that we still had nowhere to live. One day I threw myself across their bed and burst into tears. They came in to comfort me, each in their own way—Kathy with a hug and Jim with a challenging but necessary word.

While Kathy held me, Jim asked, "What's the matter, Sue?"

"What do you mean, what's the matter? We don't have anywhere to live!"

"Do you have food?" Jim asked.

"Yes."

"Do you have clothing?"

"Yes."

"Do you have shelter?"

(Sniff) "Yes."

"Do you have fellowship?"

"Yes."

"Then what's the problem?"

"I want my own house!"

Then Jim said tenderly, "I see your tears, and God does, too. He will give you the desires of your heart in His perfect timing. He loves you and your family very much."

They left me alone to pray. Someone at church had stated casually that the reason Loren and I didn't have a home was obviously because we had some great sin in our lives and hadn't repented. So I asked God which sin was holding back His blessing. I heard a gentle but firm answer, "This is not a punishment; it is for My glory. Are you willing to go through with it?"

I wanted it to be over. I wanted a house!—but not until God had done whatever He was doing in our lives. I knew He could show us the house now, but as Jim said, it wasn't yet His perfect timing. I also realized that finding the house had become all-consuming and taken on a life of its own. The house had become my god. So I decided I wasn't going to look anymore until God directed me to do so.

There was peace. After a week with Jim and Kathy, Loren

and I received a call from Leslie, our former next-door neighbor, who told us that her father-in-law had died and they needed to leave town right away. Did we want to housesit?

Moving into their house was almost like moving back into our own. It was hard being back in the neighborhood because everyone knew we were homeless; all our belongings were still sitting out front in the truck. (Keith corrected me later and said, "We were never homeless; we just didn't have a house. If we were together, we were home.")

It was also hard to stay next door to our old house when it was filled with a new family and we still had no place to call our own. I met the new owner and she invited me in. At first it was like sticking a knife in my heart, but when I walked in and saw how nicely it was decorated with antiques, it didn't even look familiar. I was finally able to let go. It wasn't our home anymore and it really was going to be okay.

That was the beginning of the blessing God had in store for us. As I let go, He was able to begin to fill us with the new thing He was about to do.

That evening Maria called, asking for permission to share our situation with a friend of hers, who was a real estate agent. Loren and I agreed.

The next day I went to visit my sister and the kittens. I went alone since the kids were with two of their 52 friends. On the way, I felt a nudge to go look for a house, but pushed the thought aside since I was sure it was just me letting the compulsion take over again. I arrived at Diane's house, stayed for ten minutes and blurted out, "I've got to go!" Concerned, she asked me where I was going. I told her I was going to find my house.

I drove about ten miles down the road when I heard, "Turn right." I turned right and went down two streets and heard,

"Turn right." There, sitting high on a hill was a beautiful white house with pillars. I didn't see anything to indicate that it was for rent, but I started laughing and crying at the same time. I didn't know how God was going to pull it off, but I knew without a doubt that I was looking at our new home. It was huge and much more than I would ever have dared to dream. God had given that vision to Maria so I would recognize it when I found it.

As I pulled into the driveway to turn around, I noticed a *For Sale* sign which had been hidden by a large tree when I first pulled in front of the house. I was disappointed that it was not a rental, but I wrote down the address and phone number anyway and hurried back to Leslie's house, our temporary home. Cheryl had returned from visiting with her friends. As we walked into the house together, with me clutching the phone number in my hand, I heard the phone ringing. It was Maria calling to tell me that, if we wanted, we had an appointment the next day with an agent in her friend's office who owned a house. He knew all about us and was willing to work with us.

I knew I wasn't reacting as Maria expected, but I felt confused since I was convinced I had already found the house God was leading us to. But then Maria read the address of where we were to meet the owner. It was the same house I had just found on the hill! I started screaming with excitement and Maria joined in. We were in awe of the miraculous guidance and provision of the Lord. Even before I had a chance to call about that house, Loren and I had an appointment with its owner.

I hung up the phone, grabbed Cheryl and started dancing all over the house. She had no idea what was going on, but it must have been fun for her to see me so happy again.

We met with the owner and started moving into our beautiful new home the very next day. The house had been empty for the entire duration of our wandering. We could have moved in at any time, but our hearts weren't ready to receive the full extent of God's blessing until that very moment.

Acts 17:26–29 tells us, "From one man he made every nation of men, that they should inhabit the whole earth; and he determined the times set for them and *the exact places where they should live*. God did this so that men would seek him and perhaps reach out for him and find him, though he is not far from each one of us. 'For in him we live and move and have our being'" (emphasis added).

Oh, how we loved our new home! There was no denying that God had done a miracle and all who saw it gave Him glory.

SEEING GOD IN THE EVERYDAY

One year to the day that we moved into our new home, Loren got a phone call from a man he had met on the job. Loren had told me about Dave before. He called him a "gentle giant." He was well over six feet tall, could break up concrete with a single swing of the sledgehammer and could pour concrete like a piece of art. Dave unashamedly loved the Lord. And now he was on the phone.

When Loren hung up, he told me that the house where Dave and his family had been staying had been condemned for no heat. Well-meaning friends had called the county to force the landlord to fix the problem. The landlord told them he didn't care—just condemn the place. They did, and now Dave and his family had nowhere to live. Loren had told him if he ever needed anything, just give us a call (sound familiar?), so now he was calling for prayer.

I asked Loren where they were planning to stay and he told me they had nowhere to go. I said, "Oh yes, they do," and they moved in with us that night.

I had never met Dave or his family before, but we wasted

no time in becoming like family. His wife, Lovie (a great name for her!), had a strong faith like her husband, but she was clearly struggling with their circumstances. I told her I understood. She said that I couldn't understand what it felt like to be homeless. I told her what someone wise once told me: She wasn't homeless; she just didn't have a house. As long as they were together, they were home. And I told her all about God's faithfulness in bringing us to the very home she was presently standing in and how God's faithfulness would see them through as well. We could comfort with the comfort we had received.

We had a great time together. They had a daughter Keith's age, a son Cheryl's age, and a little one on the way. We were on a great adventure in our own home. We learned so much from each other. But their five-year-old son Davey probably taught me the most.

As you recall, I grew up going to Catholic school. Every Friday during Lent, we attended church as a class for the Stations of the Cross, a service remembering the journey of Jesus leading to the cross. Every week, when others were bored and yawning, I would start crying when we came to the part where Veronica wiped the face of Jesus and again when Jesus died on the cross. Every week! I didn't know what was wrong with me, but I couldn't keep the tears from falling.

Now, all these years later, I longed to go back to the Stations of the Cross. So I went back to the church of my childhood.

I was sure I wouldn't cry when Veronica wiped the face of Jesus this time because, after all, I thought I was enlightened, plus I knew that particular story wasn't even in the Bible. Like so many other things, they had changed the practice since I last sat in the very same pew as an eighth-grader. Previously, the

69

priest would pray and read a story depicting what was happening to Jesus on His way to the cross. Then the congregation would respond in prayer before moving to the next plaque. Now, they read Scripture in lieu of the story.

I wondered what Scripture they would read for Veronica since it wasn't in the Bible. And then, sure enough, tears began to flow. As a child, I had wanted to wipe the face of Jesus just as Veronica had done, but I knew I would never have the opportunity. As I pondered this, the priest began to read:

"'Come, you who are blessed by my Father; take your inheritance, the kingdom prepared for you since the creation of the world. For I was hungry and you gave me something to eat, I was thirsty and you gave me something to drink, I was a stranger and you invited me in, I needed clothes and you clothed me, I was sick and you looked after me, I was in prison and you came to visit me.'

"Then the righteous will answer him, 'Lord, when did we see you hungry and feed you, or thirsty and give you something to drink? When did we see you a stranger and invite you in, or needing clothes and clothe you? When did we see you sick or in prison and go to visit you?'

"The King will reply, 'I tell you the truth, whatever you did for one of the least of these brothers of mine, you did for me.'"

Matthew 25:34–40

I had cried all those years ago because my heart understood what my mind could not grasp. I cried now because my mind finally understood what my heart had known all along. Every day was an opportunity to wipe the face of Jesus. That very morning, little Davey had gotten sick. I had knelt

70

down next to him by the toilet and wiped his face with a damp cloth while he vomited. It may not sound holy or particularly spiritual, but I had wiped the face of Jesus.

Seeing God in the everyday is simply opening our hearts and eyes to how He reveals Himself through the ordinary moments of our lives. It is looking for Him in everyday events. It is becoming aware of opportunities to serve Him through serving others. It's falling in love with Jesus.

Dave's family moved into their new God-given home, but they never moved out of our hearts. Both families are grateful recipients of God's amazing provision and grace.

THE BOX

It never ceases to amaze me how God can take two people from different countries, cultures and backgrounds and meld their lives together so completely. That's the gift He has given me through my friend Maria. Every Wednesday for eighteen years (and now via phone), we gathered for prayer. We shared life's joys and sorrows, our marriages, the lives of our children and all those we love. We prayed over health concerns, family tragedies, fears, victories and, most especially, our faith. We laughed so hard we cried and we cried so hard we healed. In a very real sense, Maria is my soul mate and I treasure her friendship.

Those Wednesdays were a breath of life for both of us. We always pointed each other to Jesus, and were amazed how, even if nothing had changed, everything was different after prayer. We helped each other see things through the eyes of God.

There was one long summer when, due to vacations and activities with our children, Maria and I hadn't seen each other in several weeks. Once the kids were back in school, we hungrily set aside a day to catch up and pray together.

She told me what she and her family had experienced

since we last met, and I did the same. But when I finished sharing, she asked, "What's *really* going on?" She never let me get away with anything. Though it may not always be comfortable, it is a true blessing to be known so well and loved anyway. That's what friends do best.

The truth was simple; I had been deeply hurt by something someone very close had said to me. I laughed at the time, as a defense mechanism, and it became an inside joke every time we were together. But every time, it dug a little deeper, and so did my resentment. I was tired of being the super Christian with a big smile on my face. It had hurt, and I was angry. And now I was miserable.

As she often did, Maria listened and then took both my hands into hers. She bowed her head and began to pray. As she prayed, a vision slowly began to take shape. I saw a huge box, beautifully wrapped in white paper and tied with a glistening bow. I was excited because it was a gift I was giving to God. As He began to open it, I suddenly became aware of the words Maria was praying: "Father, we give to You all our pain, disappointment and self-pity. We give to You our resentment, anger, pride and hatred."

It was then that I saw the contents of the box. With each word Maria prayed, God pulled out a matching emotion. He showed me that I had given Him pain, disappointment, self-pity, resentment, anger, pride and hatred. I was so ashamed. I cried out to Him, "I'm sorry, Lord. I wanted to give You something beautiful, but all I have is this ugliness in my heart."

His answer came softly, "Then you don't understand. You *have* given Me a beautiful gift. When you gave Me these things that weighed you down, what's left behind is a clean heart, which is precious in My sight."

Sometimes we all need a little help to see things from

God's perspective. Forgiveness is a beautiful thing; the forgiveness we receive from Him as well as the forgiveness we offer others who have offended us. When we finally glimpse and embrace that heavenly truth, everything is genuinely different.

"Create in me a clean heart, O God, and put a new and right spirit within me" (Psalm 51:10, NRSV).

THE GIFT GOES ON

I t was going to be the best Christmas ever! It was early December, all our bills were paid, and there was money left over. I didn't know where it came from, but it didn't matter. All I knew was, we had enough money to replace our black-and-white, three-working-channel television set with a new color TV! The kids would love it. I could picture it under the Christmas tree with a shiny red bow. Nothing could prevent us from rushing out and buying that coveted box of entertainment ... except the love of God.

Getting a new TV was a big deal for us. Loren and I studied the different brands. We even reserved a babysitter so we could go shopping for it together. We were about to go on our big adventure when the phone rang. My sister Diane was calling to tell me about her friend's troubles and to ask for prayer.

This woman had one child, was pregnant with another, and her husband had left her with nothing. She had been going to a clinic for her prenatal care. The nurse had told her that day that she had to pay the bill in full before they would admit her for delivery. It wasn't that much, but she had no way of getting the money. She was desperate. She even considered an abortion.

My heart hurt for her. If she couldn't even pay for the delivery, how could she afford to keep the baby? I promised Diane to keep her friend in my prayers, hung up the phone and left with Loren for our shopping date.

But my heart wasn't in it. I found no pleasure in looking at television sets. Loren and I sat and talked over coffee about what we could do to help this hurting family. We both knew what God was asking of us. He wanted us to use His money for a child instead of a TV.

It was Christmas time and I envisioned Mary pregnant with Jesus. She was unwed, facing the possibility of being rejected by Joseph and being stoned to death. But she was carrying the Child of God and their heavenly Father would take care of them.

Then I imagined what this young mother was going through and knew she was carrying a child of God, too. He would also take care of them. He would provide. This time He chose to use us.

Loren and I got the information from my sister and went to the clinic to pay the bill. We spoke to the nurse and asked her not to tell who we were, but just to tell the woman that God loved her and her child.

We learned later that when the mother went in for her next visit, the nurse excitedly handed her the chart, marked boldly *Paid in Full.* She not only gave her our message of God's love, but she gave her His message of hope as well. The nurse, herself a believer, shared the gospel with her.

The love of the Lord provides not only for our physical needs, but for our spiritual needs as well. If we are willing to accept His free gift of grace, then our debt is "Paid in Full" and we can be born again and receive the right to be called children of God. On Christmas morning the Child was born. On an afternoon called Good Friday, the Man died. On Easter morning the King rose victoriously. And for all eternity the Gift goes on.

We woke up Christmas morning to no TV decorated with a big red bow under the tree. The children ran down the stairs to find a Muppets™ drum set and a Rainbow-Brite™ tent instead. As they reached the bottom step, they shouted out in unison, "This is the best Christmas ever!"

No truer words were ever spoken.

THE ZOO

My family and I experienced a wonderful time at a four-day Christian camp one summer. We enjoyed concerts by the dozens, with teachings, worship and fellowship with approximately five thousand other believers every day. It was a great adventure, but it was hot—really, really hot. There was not a shade tree to be found anywhere. I drank large amounts of water and juice, but it wasn't enough. I got sick—really, really sick. We had to go home early. But once I cooled off in the air conditioning and drank more water, I felt fine.

So, when my sister called the next day to invite me and my children to go to the National Zoo with her and her children, I didn't think anything of it. We went and had a great time—for about half an hour. It was another scorcher of a day. We were standing in line for drinks when my legs gave out and I fainted. Someone called security and they carried me to their only air-conditioned building, the Reptile House, and put me upstairs in the office with lizards until an ambulance could get there. I was scared upstairs, and Diane and the kids were scared downstairs. Then the ambulance arrived and carried me to the hospital. Diane followed close behind in her car, fearing she would lose us through busy streets of Washington, D.C.

I thought I was dying. I was convinced I had some type of rare disease. It actually turned out to be food poisoning and dehydration. But the Lord was on duty in the ambulance that day, and suddenly I forgot I was sick.

There were three EMTs taking care of me—one driving, one riding up front, and the other in the back with me. While stopped at a red light, the driver slid the little window open and said, "Hey, Tony, did you realize you've been riding with us for a year now?"

In response to this tiny morsel of information, I simply said, "Happy anniversary!"

Tony looked at me with wonder in his eyes and asked, "How did you know?"

"How did I know what?"

He said, "How did you know that today is my fifth anniversary, but my wife left me a week ago?"

God can use the smallest window of opportunity to minister hope to those in need. Tony was trembling as he told me the whole story.

Lying on that cot, I spoke to him about God's love and the hope of reconciliation. I told him that I didn't know anything, but that God knew everything about him, everything about his situation, and that He cared, He truly cared.

It was a 25-minute drive to the hospital through the winding one-way streets and traffic of Washington, D.C. I was grateful for every minute I had to share with this dear man. Before we arrived at the hospital, Tony knelt down beside my cot and gave his life to the Lord, repenting and asking for grace and guidance. He turned it all over to Jesus and asked Him into his heart.

Needless to say, I had a better ride than Diane. As they rolled me into a hospital room, I passed her and the kids in the hall, assuring them I was going to be okay. I was glowing; Diane was sweating. The poor woman had been frantically following the ambulance in a car filled with crying kids, not knowing what was wrong with me. At that point, I think I could have tried to look a little sicker for her sake.

I spent the next four hours hooked up to machines and drinking gallons of my least favorite sports drink. A small price to pay for a soul saved that day.

For some strange reason, Diane and I never went on many outings together after that, but I know God received her sacrifice of love and turned it into power for His Kingdom. Her reward will be great. The zoo could wait, but Tony could not.

FALSE ALARM?

I f you're not careful, things can get boring in the life cycle of marriage and family. It's up to you to keep it interesting. It is also easy for couples to get lost in the roles of parenthood. You marry, have kids who become your entire life, watch them grow up and leave home, and then you're stuck with a perfect stranger. In order to prevent this from happening, Loren and I instituted a "date night."

We were blessed with family and friends who would watch the kids for a few hours each week while we went off to be together, just the two of us. We didn't have much money, but that didn't matter. Sometimes we'd play tennis, or go for a walk in the park, or go to the airport to "people watch." But every now and then, we would splurge and go out to dinner.

On one such evening, we went to our favorite Chinese restaurant, tucked away in the middle of a small strip mall. We had developed a friendship with the owners and they treated us like family, which makes this story even more difficult.

As we were enjoying our candlelight dinner, a fire alarm was suddenly blaring in the mall. As I looked around, no one seemed fazed. Everyone kept chatting and eating their meals. We were sitting near the window, so I observed people

81

standing in line at the movie theater and others shopping in the card store. Why wasn't anyone moving? Why wasn't anyone concerned?

"Come on," I said to Loren. "Let's go outside to the parking lot." He mentioned that no one else seemed too worried, but I insisted. I would feel ridiculous if we died in a fire because we ignored the alarm. (Don't think too far into the logic of that last statement.)

So we left our meal on the table and went out to the parking lot. Three fire engines, with lights flashing, were parked near the theater. We walked over and asked a fireman about the situation. He told us there was a small electrical fire in the projection room. I asked, "Shouldn't everyone be getting out of the building?" He said if there was a need to evacuate, they would announce it and get the people out. I stated that it was my impression that was exactly the purpose of a fire alarm. In an uncharacteristic reaction for a fireman, he laughed. I didn't think it was funny.

They extinguished the fire and told everyone it was safe to go back inside. (That would be just the two of us.) When Loren and I sat back down at our table, our waiter came over and said, "We were worried. It's not like you to leave without paying. Where did you go?" I told him we had gone outside because of the fire alarm. Then he joked, "Oh, sure, you were safe and you were going to leave us all in here to burn?" I replied with a broken heart, "You heard the same warning!"

The experience really shook me. I couldn't sleep that night. The scene kept replaying over again in my mind, and the waiter's words were ringing in my ear. I went to the Lord in prayer and heard these words from Matthew 24:37: "As it was in the days of Noah, so it will be at the coming of the Son of Man."

God warned Noah of the flood to come, and even though it didn't make sense, by faith, Noah believed God and built the ark. Matthew continues, "For in the days before the flood, people were eating and drinking [and going to the movies and buying greeting cards], marrying and giving in marriage, up to the day Noah entered the ark; and they knew nothing about what would happen until the flood came and took them all away" (verses 38–39). They didn't know because they weren't listening. They didn't heed the warning, and then it was too late.

Sadly, our culture is dulling us to warning signs as well. It is actually conditioning us to ignore them, as evidenced by the fireman's lack of concern for the alarm. Yet, the Lord is calling us to keep watch.

We are not to live our lives in fear, but in preparedness for the Lord's return. I want those I love to hear the warnings and obey. That's why the waiter's words were so haunting. The thought of leaving others behind breaks my heart. But I can't make anyone follow. I can only tell them of the Lord's invitation; they must choose to accept it.

Our kids are now adults, but Loren and I still enjoy our date nights. We delight in going out to eat at a good restaurant; we go to the movies and eat buttered popcorn; and I should own stock in a card shop. We are happy and enjoy life as we eagerly await Jesus' triumphant reappearance on earth.

The foretold return of our Savior is not merely a warning; it is a promise that will one day be fulfilled. Our hope is in Jesus. Please listen to Him.

DR. HOPE

For two weeks I lay flat on my back in unbearable pain. I had dropped a pencil on the floor at work, and when I bent down to pick it up, I felt a searing pain, like a knife piercing the base of my neck. The pain only intensified with time. My husband rushed me to the doctor where I was quickly diagnosed with a herniated disk pressing against my spinal cord and causing me to lose the use of my left arm. I was told I needed surgery or risked losing the use of my arm altogether. Unfortunately, the earliest the doctor could operate was two weeks away. And so, I lay in bed unable to move. And then, like a nightmare, on the day I was scheduled for surgery, I awoke with a fiery throat infection. The operation had to be postponed for another two weeks. I didn't know how I was going to endure it.

My mind drifted back to when Cheryl was a little girl. She had fallen out of a tree house and landed flat on her back. In my panic, I picked her up and ran next door. My neighbor was a nurse, and when she opened the door, I begged her to fix Cheryl. We called an ambulance. The x-rays showed that she had a fractured collarbone, so they put her arm in a sling for six weeks. When we got home, Loren, Keith and I prayed over her.

The next day she started complaining about the sling. She didn't want to wear it; her arm didn't hurt anymore. After three days, her resistance to the sling grew, so I took her back to the doctor. They took another x-ray and were amazed when they compared it to the first one. God had done a miracle; there was no sign of the fracture that had been there just three days ago. The break was completely healed. We were surprised, but Cheryl was not. She knew she had been healed instantly, but it took us three days to believe her. She had the faith of a child; we had prayed, but she had believed God would do what we asked.

I knew God could heal me, too. But what happens when healing doesn't come about right away and the situation only intensifies? Is God any less faithful? If He doesn't calm the storm that is raging against us, we can be sure He will calm the storm raging within us.

I know this to be true because of lessons learned during my extended waiting period. A friend called to cheer me up, saying, "I know this must be difficult, but can you see God working in all this?"

I said, "No."

She said, "I mean, can you hear God speaking to you?"

I said, "No."

Disheartened, she asked, "Can you at least feel Him there with you? Are you using this time in prayer for others?"

I said, "No. I wish it were so, but I am in excruciating pain, and I don't think He's expecting much out of me right now. But just because I can't see Him, hear Him or feel Him doesn't mean He isn't here. He promised to never leave me or forsake me, and I have no reason to doubt His presence with me now."

We were both cheered by the reality of Immanuel, "God

with us." My childlike faith knew absolutely that He would never leave me in my time of need.

My faith wasn't tested; it was proved.

Later that day our pastor came over to pray and anoint my head with fragrant oil. When he left, a peace washed over me. I praised God and said, "Thank You, Lord. Even though I can't see You or hear You or feel You, I can *smell* You." By faith, I basked in the fragrance of my ever-present God and I was satisfied.

Two weeks later, God brought complete healing. This time He chose to use a surgeon. The doctor's name was yet another confirmation of the loving care of my Healer and Great Physician; his name was Dr. Hope. "And we rejoice in the hope of the glory of God. Not only so, but we also rejoice in our sufferings, because we know that suffering produces perseverance; perseverance, character; and character, hope. And hope does not disappoint us, because God has poured out his love into our hearts by the Holy Spirit, whom he has given us" (Romans 5:2–5).

Our God is an ever-faithful God. The pain I had known was temporary; His love, everlasting. Hope had tenderly carried me through this time of suffering.

SERVANT OF GOD

I woke up on my birthday and felt the sweet presence of the Lord very near. I could almost hear Him ask me what I wanted for my birthday. It didn't take long for me to search for the deep desire of my heart. "O Lord, I want to be free from the IRS!"

My husband is a skilled craftsman. He has owned his own home improvement company for many years. Up to this point of the story, that had meant many years of financial hardship. "Harsh winter" meant much more than a seasonal forecast to us. Many winters Loren had little or no work. We went from one crisis to another. And out of that hardship, a ten-year ordeal with the IRS ensued.

At the end of one year, we didn't have enough money to pay the Social Security tax. The IRS agent told us it was no problem; we could pay it later, incurring penalty and interest. That was easy, so the next year we found ourselves in the same situation. No problem—more penalty and interest. Then we were put on a payment plan—again, no problem—during the summer. When the next winter hit hard, we had no money to spare and didn't keep up with the payment plan.

Now there was a problem! The IRS began wiping out our

checking account without notice. All the checks we wrote to cover our bills began to bounce, bringing about even more penalties. The IRS put us on another payment plan, but we couldn't keep up. Eventually they threatened to take everything we owned. Ours was a life of shame. For me it took the shape of fear. For Loren it was a sense of failure. We became, in every sense of the word, slaves to the IRS. What started out as a $3,000 debt was now $120,000. There seemed no way of escape.

We all love to hate the IRS, but Romans 13:1 tells us that "everyone must submit himself to the governing authorities" because they have been established by God. If we do good, Paul writes, we don't have to worry. But if we do wrong, we should be afraid. He is "God's servant to do us good," but he is also "an agent of wrath to bring punishment on the wrongdoer" (verse 4). We are then told, "This is also why you pay taxes, for the authorities are God's servants" (verse 6).

We had done wrong.

I remember saying to the Lord, "I understand why You can't bail us out of this one. We would never learn our lesson. It's okay; we'll work it out. After all, this sin is our fault." The Holy Spirit replied, "Which one isn't? They are all your fault, but that's never stopped My forgiveness or grace before. Give it to Me."

And we did.

We met with our IRS agent again and told him we were wrong and that we wanted to make it right but we didn't know how. We told him he was a servant of God in our lives and that we needed help. He told us he had been called a lot of things in his years as an IRS agent, but *never* a "servant of God"! He would try to work with us.

And that was a turning point in our lives. The agent came

to our home and made us an "Offer and Compromise" which the IRS had set up for just such cases. They agreed to accept $16,000, and they would forgive the balance—which was the penalty and interest due—with the understanding that we would remain current in our taxes. We had thirty days to come up with the money.

We accepted gratefully, knowing that, in reality, $16,000 was the same as $120,000—just as impossible for us, but not for God.

Loren and I felt strongly that the Lord was instructing us to tell no one about the "Offer and Compromise" or ask anyone for help. We were not to lean on our own resources, but wait for Him and He would do a miracle. He would send someone who would ask specifically about our situation with the IRS, and only with that one person could we share.

With only three weeks left until the payment was due, I woke up from the ten-year nightmare to the sweet sound of Jesus asking me, "What do you want for your birthday?" I replied, "O Lord, I want to be free from the IRS!"

On this, my birthday, friends from church had gathered in the park to celebrate a baby shower for a mutual friend. It was a beautiful day in April, and when the party was over, I stood alone on a little bridge, mindlessly dropping sticks into the water below, watching them float away. I was alone with my thoughts when a dear friend of many years who had attended the baby shower came up to chat. We talked about many things. Then she asked if the situation with the IRS had ever cleared up. My heart leaping, I told her everything. She listened, consoled me and quietly walked away, leaving me alone once again with my thoughts.

I lay in bed that night thankful for God's promise, but disappointed that nothing had happened. It was the end of my birthday and we were still not free from the debt we owed.

A week went by and still nothing changed. It was hard to not take matters into our own hands. The due date was getting uncomfortably close.

The next day the phone rang, and my friend from the party asked if she and her husband could come over. Without warning or fanfare, they sat across from us at the kitchen table and handed us a check for $20,000. Just like that, the ordeal was over. I didn't know it, but we also owed $4,000 for our state tax. God knew the exact amount we needed to break the bondage of debt, and He used these dear saints to unshackle the chains. His grace and their kindness and obedience changed our lives. Loren actually felt the physical oppression leave as he wrote the check to the IRS.

Years of suffering and shame vanished in an instant. God's grace is sufficient. We didn't deserve it; we never do. But it was God's good pleasure to set our feet on a new course of freedom.

Over the next five years, we paid our friends back with no interest. It wasn't free, but it was freeing.

Know this: If you experience a place of shame, He is the lifter of your head. If you find yourself in a situation from which there seems to be no way out, the Lord is your Deliverer and delights in setting His people free.

We are sinners; He is the Redeemer. We are the servants forgiven a great debt; He is the King who forgives. We are called to worship Him with our lives, and that includes how we handle our money. With all our hearts, we want to be found trustworthy in handling worldly wealth so He can trust us with true riches. Jesus said, "Give to Caesar what is Caesar's, and to God what is God's" (Matthew 22:21). Our taxes belong to the IRS, but our lives belong to Him!

PERFECT TIMING

L oren and I were supposed to go to the beach for a
romantic getaway. However, he arrived home from
work late, we went out to eat late, and it gets dark early in the
fall. We only drove about eight miles down the road and
stopped at a way-too-local hotel for the night. It was almost
like getting away. The next morning we decided to go to
Skyline Drive in the Blue Ridge Mountains instead of the
beach. While it would have taken four hours to get to the
beach, the mountains were only an hour away.

We took a nap on a blanket on top of a sunny hill. Then we
began our journey to Dark Hollow Falls. As we were walking
down, I was getting more and more concerned about the people
who were coming up. They were all huffing and puffing and
looked like they were on the verge of heart attacks. I wasn't so
sure I could make it. Loren suggested that I ask the next person
we passed how much farther to the falls and if they thought it
was worth the trip.

Two women approached. I asked them the questions and
they assured us that it was well worth the trip. As they passed,
Loren asked me if I knew with whom I had just spoken—our
English teacher from our junior year in high school! I called

out her name and she turned with a puzzled look on her face and came toward us. I asked if she remembered us. I reminded her that my maiden name was Sue Donohue.

Her face paled. "Sue Donohue? I can't believe it's you! I can't tell you how many times through the years I have thought of you and wondered what happened to you. You helped me keep my sanity back then. As a matter of fact, just two weeks ago, I was talking to a friend and telling her how I wished I had kept in touch with some of my students, and if I could only find one, it would be Sue Donohue! I even considered going by your house to see if your parents still lived there and asking them where you were. And here you are standing in front of me. I can't believe it! What have you been doing all these years?"

I filled her in with the details of our life.

She turned to Loren and asked, "Was I your teacher, too?"

Loren said, "Yes."

Her head hung low. "Was I mean to you?"

"Well ... "

Full of remorse, she asked, "Did I fail you?"

"The only F I received in my high school career," Loren responded.

"Did you fail for the year? Did you not graduate because of me?"

"No," Loren said, "I passed with a D."

She looked into Loren's eyes and said she was sorry, that she knew she had been unkind and unreasonable back then but that she had mellowed out over the years. She told us stories of running into former students who were afraid of her and hated her. It was sad.

Loren reassured her. We invited her over for dinner; then we all hugged and went our separate ways.

After we parted, Loren and I walked down to Dark Hollow Falls. They were right; it was unquestionably worth it. As we sat by the water, we prayed for this special woman. Many things amazed us about that encounter. First of all, it wouldn't have happened if we had gone to the beach or if we hadn't taken a nap on the sunny hill before going on our hike. God's timing was perfect! Second, she had been "searching" for me, but when we spoke, she didn't realize I was the one standing in front of her, nor did I recognize her. The Lord used Loren to bring us together. How many times do we search for God's answer to a prayer and not recognize Him until someone else reveals Him to us?

I remembered the fear I had had, as a junior in high school, when I got my schedule and saw that she was going to be my teacher. I had heard horrible stories about her. But I decided that no one could be *that* bad, and that she deserved a chance. I would make up my own mind about her and not listen to anyone else. We clicked. We loved each other. For whatever reason, I could see something in her that few others saw.

As Loren and I sat by the water, my heart was touched by how much one life could affect another without even knowing it. I knew at that moment that the Lord had allowed me to love the unlovable back then because He had a plan for her now. I saw clearly that the love I had shared with her in high school was the open door He was using in the present—and that Loren held true power in the ministry of reconciliation for her past. He represented all the kids who had been hurt. Our hugs embodied both love and forgiveness. And I absolutely knew she wasn't looking for me; she was searching for the love that I symbolized. She was longing to be loved, and Loren and I knew Love Himself. We had something to teach our teacher because we knew the love of the Father.

God is in control. He can take the dark hollow places of our souls and bring the light of His love to fill every void. He is always enough.

BLUEBERRY PIE

How glorious it is when old friends get together to fellowship in the Lord! Our dear friend and teacher Jeff was in town and the old crew gathered at a local restaurant. We walked in with Bibles, so, amazingly enough, a new seating section opened up in the back room. That was okay with us. We spent hours laughing, talking, sharing and catching up.

While we were lost in the joy of togetherness, a lone man was seated in the corner. He looked rather odd and fidgety. When his food came, he ate it quickly—I mean *really* fast— never putting down his fork or, it seemed, even slowing down to swallow. I didn't mean to stare, but I couldn't help but notice him.

As he was finishing his meal, we were ordering dessert. Jeff asked the waitress to take a piece of blueberry pie to the man in the corner and put it on our tab. The gentleman glanced up once and looked our way as he inhaled the pie. Then, after he finished, he walked over to our table with his head down and eyes fixed on the floor.

"Th-th-thank you for the-the-the pie."

It was one of the worst stutters I had ever heard. We

invited him to join us. He wouldn't sit down, but said, "Ca-ca-can I as-as-ask you a que-que-quest-question?"

We welcomed the conversation.

"Do-do-do you he-he-hear voi-voi-voices in your h-h-head?"

Okay, not the question I was expecting!

We invited him once again to sit down and then he joined us at the table.

We all did our part in sharing the freedom we knew in Jesus—the freedom that could be his. We talked about hearing the voice of God. We spoke truth to him and he listened intently. I had a little pocket Bible in my purse that I gave him to keep after underlining these verses:

"The watchman opens the gate for him, and the sheep listen to his voice. He calls his own sheep by name and leads them out. When he has brought out all his own, he goes on ahead of them, and his sheep follow him because they know his voice. But they will never follow a stranger; in fact, they will run away from him because they do not recognize a stranger's voice."

John 10:3–5

We prayed for him to receive the gift of salvation, the gift of the Holy Spirit and for freedom from the torture in his mind. He was filled with peace. His face changed. His spirit changed. His eyes shimmered with joy. And, there was one more stunning change. When he accepted the grace of God, his stutter disappeared completely. Completely! He thanked us, he thanked God and he practically danced out the door.

Needless to say, we were ecstatic. Our faith was built up, too.

That would have been enough, but God had more blessings to bestow. My friend Kathy and I excused ourselves to visit the restroom. The waitress followed us in and told us that she had been watching while those at our table talked and prayed with that man. Apparently, he came in every night and they always put him in the back room because people were afraid of him. She saw what happened. She wondered how we did it. We assured her that God had done it, and she asked if we would pray for her. She wanted God in her life, too. She accepted the Lord right there on the bathroom floor. She also asked for prayer for her daughter, who had severe learning disabilities and needed to get into a special school. It was our delight and honor to pray with her. What an awesome God we serve!

Such a simple act of kindness, a piece of blueberry pie, yet God used it to change lives—all of ours. How sweet and glorious it is when old friends get together to fellowship in the Lord!

THE BACK-TO-SCHOOL BLUES

It happened every year about this time. First came the back-to-school commercials with excited children and great deals. Then came the dreams of buying new outfits and school supplies for my own children. Keith and Cheryl had graduated from school years ago, but they were instantly transported back to childhood in my sleep-induced imagination. This was always followed by a deep sadness that washed over me, bringing a fresh and raw realization that I would never buy another protractor as long as I lived.

After five years of sighing through August, my wise and patient husband finally said, "Sue, go find a kid!" It never dawned on me that I could bless another child with school supplies.

At 9:02 the next morning, I answered the church office phone. The woman on the other end asked if the church had a program for providing school supplies to needy children. I responded, "No, but meet me at the store at 5:00 tonight and I'll take you and your children shopping." I was elated! God had heard my prayer. I didn't even have time to go find a kid; three kids had found me!

At 5:00 sharp, I walked into the store and discovered that

the woman had already started shopping without me. She was alone. There were no children with her and she was drunk. I was devastated.

She had put three backpacks into her cart, each individually costing $75. I told her we wouldn't be purchasing those particular bags, but that she could choose three other ones from the less expensive rack. I asked to see the required list from the school and she showed it to me reluctantly. She kept throwing extras into the cart and I kept taking them out. She yelled at the store clerk and I followed close behind, apologizing. She asked if she could get a computer. I said no. She asked if she could at least get a printer, and I asked her what she would do with a printer if she didn't have a computer. Things weren't going well.

Finally, mission accomplished, we had found three sets of everything on the list. As we were standing in line, I clearly heard the Lord whisper to my heart, "I want you to share the gospel with her and tell her that I love her." I said, "I don't want to."

As we placed the supplies on the checkout counter, He told me again, more firmly this time, "Share the gospel and tell her that I love her." It was not a suggestion. I was really struggling with anger when the woman looked up at me and said sheepishly, "I forgot the protractor." My heart melted.

We stood in the parking lot for more than an hour. She was upset that the church wouldn't buy her a computer. I explained that "the church" wasn't paying for this. Though I am part of God's church, this was coming out of my own pocket and I couldn't afford to buy her a computer. There was no program; this was a personal gift. When she finally understood that she wasn't dealing with an institution, her sense of entitlement disappeared. She expressed wonder that I would do this for a perfect stranger. It was simply an interaction between two needy souls that day.

I explained how God had brought us together and why I needed her as much as she needed me. Her heart melted, as mine had done moments earlier. I told her that God loved her, to which she responded, "Sometimes I drink." I assured her that He knew and loved her anyway. The good news was that Jesus had come to set her free.

She said she wasn't a good mother; I told her He was a good Father.

She said she didn't deserve His love; I told her it was pure grace.

She claimed that if I knew her I wouldn't say such things; I told her that God knew her and that such things were not dependent upon her behavior but on His character. Forgiveness was hers for the taking. The Lord offered it in full awareness of why she needed it.

All the arguments of why He shouldn't love her collapsed in the comfort of knowing it was an argument she couldn't win. God *is* love and He couldn't be convinced otherwise. We prayed together, wept together, hugged and waved goodbye.

I no longer suffer with the back-to-school-blues. My "kids" will never be young again; that's just not the way it works. But life goes on, and we have been blessed with grandchildren and others whom God brings into our lives. There are children throughout the world getting ready for the first day of school. Apparently my fear was unwarranted; there will always be someone in need of a protractor.

LOVE

"We love because he first loved us."
1 John 4:19

THE KING

We were, like so many times before, sitting in the living room of our dear friends Jim and Kathy. Jim's question was always the same: "So, what's God been teaching you lately?" Jim was never one for small talk.

Kathy shared one of my favorite stories. She and Jim had agreed that she would not work outside their home for their first year of marriage. It was difficult for Kathy's family to understand this decision.

One night her brother called and said, "So, Kathy, what are you doing now?"

She told him that she volunteered at her church, went to a Bible study, visited an elderly woman once a week, etc.

He said, "Yeah, but what are you *doing*? Are you going to school?"

"No."

"Are you working?"

"No."

"Well then, *what* are you doing?"

She had no acceptable answer for him. Although she had been in total agreement with Jim, her brother's conversation made her question their decision. After she hung up the phone, she asked the Lord angrily, "Why can't I work? Everyone works! Even Jesus had a job—He was a carpenter!"

In compassion Jesus replied, "Kathy, I'm not known for My chairs." His work was eternal—and so was the work He had given her to do.

As we let her words sink in, we all started sharing just who Jesus is, what He had done for each of us, and the different images we had of Christ. When it was my turn, I said excitedly, "Oh, I see Jesus as my Best Friend!" Jim agreed, and then he challenged me by saying that, as I grew and matured in my faith, I would come to see Him as much more; I would come to see Him as King.

My heart sank. Truthfully, I liked having Jesus as my Best Friend and didn't ever want to outgrow that feeling.

But that night in my evening prayers, I asked Jesus to reveal Himself to me as King. I knew it was time for me to grow up and desire the deeper things of God. I fell asleep and had a dream—a dream I will never forget.

There I was, kneeling before the great and glorious King. I was dressed in full armor as a soldier of the King, and I was shaking in my boots. He was sitting on His throne, dressed in royal robes with a crown upon His head. I was frightened, but somehow I summoned enough courage to chance a peek at Him. And there, looking back at me with a twinkle in His eye, was the face of my Best Friend. He rose, came toward me, touched both of my shoulders with His sword and knighted me. He was very much King, but He didn't stop being my intimate Friend.

I did grow in faith that night, but I also grew in my understanding that I will never outgrow my need for intimacy with my Best Friend. In fact, in John 15, Jesus says, "I no longer call you servants, because a servant does not know his

103

master's business. Instead, I have called you friends, for everything that I learned from my Father I have made known to you. You did not choose me, but I chose you and appointed you to go and bear fruit—fruit that will last" (verses 15 and 16).

We have been knighted for service by our Friend, the King of glory. We have a job to do. Let us be about our Father's business—not that of building chairs, but of building His Kingdom.

THE LONG WALK HOME

When I was fifteen years old, Loren and I had gone for a long walk on a hot summer night. We were both supposed to be home by ten o'clock, and it was already ten-thirty. Loren lived exactly one mile from my house, and since we were both late, I told him just to walk me halfway home; I'd be fine the rest of the way. Bad decision. No sooner had Loren disappeared around the corner than a man on a black motorcycle pulled up and stopped me. He was drunk and I was terrified.

The man told me to get on the back of the bike. I refused. He ordered me to get on the motorcycle. I refused. He pulled the motorcycle up onto the sidewalk, told me he had a gun and that I was to get on the bike now. I refused. With courage that came from someplace other than my fifteen-year-old self, I told him he could walk me home if he wanted, but that I wasn't getting on the bike with him. Amazingly, that satisfied him.

For the next hour, the guy poured out his story to a frightened teenager. His girlfriend had just broken up with him; that was why he was drinking. I told him hurting me would only make things worse. He had his whole life in front of him, and I was sure someone else would come along for him. It was strange. As long as we were talking, he was okay. If I made a sudden move, he got agitated and yelled at me—but, most of the time, he was calm.

When we were two doors down from my house, I took off running. It was probably a foolish thing to do if he really had a gun (which I now doubt, but fully believed then), but all I could think was that I wanted to get home. It was almost midnight as he sped away on his bike and I reached my house.

My parents were waiting for me in the living room. They were understandably upset and informed me emphatically that I was grounded. I stood in cold silence, unable to speak of the ordeal with the man on the motorcycle. When my parents were done, I ran downstairs and fell apart. I was standing in the middle of the basement floor, sobbing and shaking uncontrollably. My father heard me crying, so he rushed down the stairs and came to me. Fear gripped him. I still couldn't talk because I was in shock. He took me by the shoulders and pleaded with me to tell him what happened. I was finally able to tell him about the man on the motorcycle. Since only a few minutes had passed, he ran upstairs, grabbed the keys and took off after the guy.

Now I was really scared. I didn't know what my father would do if he caught him and I didn't know if the man would shoot my father. And then I felt guilty. He hadn't actually *done* anything. He threatened, but he never touched me.

Soon Dad returned to the house. He said he had seen the man take the motorcycle deep into the woods before he lost him.

We called the police. However, so much time had passed they were certain they wouldn't be able to find him. They would do a search, and if he had a gun, we would press charges. The police told me I shouldn't have been alone at night and to use more sense next time.

My father held me close after they left.

The police never found him and I was strangely relieved. It was a horrifying experience—but one I will always treasure dearly in my heart. My dad loved me. He proved it. I felt safe. I felt protected. I knew he'd lay down his own life for mine. I saw God in my father that night.

And I see that fatherly characteristic in God. I know my heavenly Father loves me. He proved it. He sent His Son to lay down His life for mine. I feel safe. I feel protected. "'Because he loves me,' says the LORD, 'I will rescue him; I will protect him, for he acknowledges my name.

I am honored and blessed to know the love of my fathers, both in heaven and on earth. I am no longer a frightened teenager in need of my father's protection. I am a grown woman wobbling through life assured of it. My confidence and peace are in Him. My dad taught me that.

LOOK WHO JESUS LOVES

When my niece was five years old, she possessed an incredible beauty. She became involved in pageants, with all the glamor and pitfalls that come with them. Although my dream of becoming Miss America never materialized, Courtney carried the family honor and proudly wore the crown of Little Miss Hawaii after winning the hearts of the judges with her charm and talent while doing the hula with poise and grace.

She went on to represent Hawaii in the Little Miss America Pageant, held that year in a very small town in Florida. We were all excited to see our brother Rich, his wife Pat and their daughter Courtney here on the mainland again. My mother, sisters and I flew to Florida to cheer her on and support the family.

Let me just say, besides the Little Miss America pageant, there was absolutely nothing going on in that town—nothing! When my sisters complained, I grabbed a blanket and marched them all outside to lie down and make pictures out of the clouds. In my way of thinking, there is never an excuse to be bored. There is either work to be done or beauty to behold, in whatever form it may be found. Cloud-watching in Florida became a treasured memory we still talk about to this day.

I admit I had some concerns for Courtney and all the little girls performing that night. It was certainly exciting, and the girls were adorable, but it caused a lot of pressure for such young ones and their parents, as well as hurt feelings to deal with for those who wouldn't win.

Shortly before show time, I found Courtney and a dozen or so other girls with their mothers in the dressing room putting on last-minute touches of makeup and hair spray. I had brought a God-inspired gift for my niece, and this was the perfect time to give it to her. It was a framed wall mirror, but one with a message revealing the source of her true beauty. My husband had hand-painted a rose along the side of the mirror with the words *Look Who Jesus Loves* in calligraphy across the top. I read it to her, and with awe in her voice, she exclaimed, "It's me! Jesus loves me!"

And with that, all the girls swarmed to look into the mirror to see if their faces would be there. Genuine surprise overtook each one when her face appeared. As they passed the mirror around, girl after girl exclaimed with pure joy, "It's me! Jesus loves me!"

It was more than I could have asked or imagined. What began as a simple gesture of encouragement for my niece became a roomful of blessing to all God's children present that day. But there was one more precious daughter of God who needed to know the truth.

Just before the girls went on stage, one mother came over to me with sadness in her eyes. It was obvious that she carried shame. "I know logically that my face has to be there," she said. "But may I see it for myself? I need to know." And with that, she took the mirror and gazed into her reflection surrounded by His words of love and compassion. Then she whispered gently, "It's me! It's true, Jesus still loves me!" She hugged the mirror to her chest and cried.

I held her in my arms and assured her that He never stopped loving her and that she was welcome back home. She looked radiant, and I realized how true it is that there is work to be done and beauty to behold, in whatever form it may be found.

Courtney didn't walk away with the crown that evening. But in a very real sense, we all received more than this world's accolades could possibly offer the moment Jesus captured our hearts with the beauty of His everlasting and unconditional love.

AND THEN THERE WERE SIX

Sometimes love can surprise us. My parents had gone through a difficult divorce, and the process was painful for all of us. Yet through the years they learned to forgive each other and get along. They spoke often on the phone. We spent every birthday, holiday, wedding and special occasion together. Eventually my father moved in with another woman who had a young son. Though we had never met them, we were cordial when speaking on the phone.

Several years passed. One day my father called a family meeting with me, my brother and three sisters, in which he revealed that Walter was not only Betty's son; he was *their* son. Dad asked for forgiveness for the pain inflicted on the family, and it was freely given. Though it was a shock, my brother, sisters and I all said the same thing: "We wish we had known all along so we could have been part of Walter's life."

We met Betty and Walter the Christmas our little brother turned nine. He looked so much like all of us that we would have recognized him on the street before we were introduced. It was strange to think that he knew all about us but that we knew little about him. We had missed so much of his childhood. When I think of my youngest sister Joanne, I imagine her on her first day of school, swinging her book bag and skipping down the sidewalk, happy as a clam and humming. There were no memories of Walter; they would have to be made in the future.

I am grateful that my father had the courage to tell us the truth about Walter when he did, because Betty died just a few months later and we were able to be there for them. After all, we were family.

Walter's presence changed our lives in big and small ways. My brother Rich was no longer my father's only son. Joanne was no longer the baby of the family. My sister Janice felt the least affected, though it undoubtedly left its mark on her life. I now had a brother three months younger than my own son.

When our children met Walter for the first time, Keith asked him, "Do we have to call you Uncle Walter?"

Walter quipped back, "No, you can call me *sir*."

For Diane, the change was enormous. She would drive an hour to Dad's home to help them through difficult days and struggles. Finally, Dad and Walter moved in with Diane and her family. She comforted them, cared for their needs and helped my father guide Walter through challenging days of mourning and confusion. She and her family sacrificed much and brought healing and wholeness back to Dad and Walter.

But what about my mother? How would she ever be able to deal with all this? It didn't take long to find out.

One day we were celebrating a birthday together at Diane's home. It was to be the first time Mom ever met Walter. She rode with us, and as we pulled up to the house, Walter came bounding out the front door and met my mother on the porch. He stuck out his hand and said, "Hi! I'm Walter; I'm Diane's brother," to which my mother replied, "Hi! I'm

Virginia; I'm Diane's mother." They hugged, and I witnessed the most precious acts of forgiveness, grace and acceptance I had ever seen. I was so proud of my mother. I decided at that very moment that she was my hero. When I grow up, I want to be just like her. She said she held no ill feelings toward the child: "He hadn't done anything wrong."

One day Walter and Dad went over to my mother's house for a visit. When Walter saw all the pictures of Mom's children and grandchildren on the back of her piano, he wondered why his picture wasn't among them. Mom tried to explain, but Walter was convinced that, if he had just been born a few years earlier, he would have been her son and his picture would also be there. So for Christmas he gave her a framed 5 x 7 print of himself, which she displayed proudly with the rest of her family. It was a cute picture of Walter, but it represented a perfect picture of God's grace.

Although there were definite changes to our family, the most important one came in the joy and new life Walter brought my father. This child needed to be loved and cared for, and my father needed to be needed. After Betty's death, Dad had to go to court to prove he was Walter's biological father. Walter's life was changed because someone loved him enough to fight for him. They shared a bond that could never be broken.

We are all looking for that same assurance that can be found so sweetly in Christ.

When I start to wonder what love looks like, I don't have to look very far; I look to my family. Janice always says, "We put the 'fun' in dys*fun*ction." Life can be messy and it doesn't always follow the right plan, but forgiveness and redemption are possible with God's help. I believe God planted me in this family to teach me how to live in love.

1 Corinthians 13:4–8 says, "Love is patient, love is kind. It does not envy, it does not boast, it is not proud. It is not rude, it is not self-seeking, it is not easily angered, it keeps no record of wrongs. Love does not delight in evil but rejoices with the truth. It always protects, always trusts, always hopes, always perseveres. Love never fails."

LESSONS OF A QUIET MAN

Grandpa Great came to live with us when he was ninety years old. Loren Van Zile, my husband's grandfather after whom he was named, had been married for 69 years before his wife died. After her death, he stopped eating and refused to take his medication. Tragedy struck again when the daughter and son-in-law he was to move in with died in a terrible accident. Grandpa was confused and didn't know what would happen to him. We asked Loren's family members if he could come live with us, as it would be very difficult for any of them to take him in. They all said no because they felt the burden would be too great. Everyone finally agreed to a three-month trial that turned into a two-year blessing.

He was supposed to move in on a Sunday afternoon. I woke up Sunday morning timid and fearful. What did I know about caring for an elderly man? My husband said simply, "Did you forget who's bringing him here?"

He was right. We hung up the huge banner the kids had made which covered the entire front of the house: *Welcome Home, Grandpa Great!* He arrived with one suitcase, an overcoat and a distinguished hat on top of his head. He handed the hat to Loren, sat in the chair facing the living room window

115

and proceeded to talk for three hours nonstop. He told us his entire life story from birth, marriage, children and career, right down to the circumstances that led to him sitting in that chair. He didn't talk again for three weeks. He had used up all his words!

People think it's amazing that we took him in (which would be normal in most cultures), and talk about how difficult it must have been for us. It wasn't difficult; it was wonderful. In fact, it was an amazing time of growth for Loren's entire family. Each came to visit or take Grandpa home with them on weekends so we could have a break when needed.

Sure, there were things that caused us to struggle. They seem petty now, but they were very real for us at the time. The children didn't like having a metal bar in their bathtub for him to hold onto for safety. I didn't want a TV in our living room and felt defiled by its presence. But Grandpa couldn't go down the stairs to the basement where we watched TV. The only other option would have been to put one in his bedroom, which would have banished him from family existence, and that would never do. So there it was, shining its eerie blue light in my living room. I hated it and had to give it to the Lord daily. But all I had to do was remember the life that came from that box—actually, the box that box came in.

Grandpa had bought a brand-new TV which arrived in a huge box (huge, at least, in my memory). We set the television up right away, but he never turned it on the whole day because there was a much better show going on in front of him. Cheryl and I spent eight hours transforming the box into a house. We cut out windows, hung curtains, painted pictures on the walls inside, built a chimney spewing white, cottony smoke, and Velcroed a shoebox—I mean mailbox—to the side of the house for important correspondence.

Grandpa sat mesmerized by all the activity. I thought we were ready for final inspection when Cheryl, who was nine years old at the time, shouted, "Wait!" and ran downstairs. She ran back upstairs with Monopoly™ money and handed it to Grandpa, saying, "Okay, Grandpa Great, you be the landlord." As he counted the money, a soothing smile crossed his face that said it all: *There is a place for me in this family.*

He had a vital role in our family. I grew to love him with all my heart. I learned much from his quiet manner. I saw what was important in life. He didn't have much—what he came with, and the only material thing that he requested to be sent to him; a grandfather clock that actually belonged to his grandfather. He said, "It must be darn near as old as I am!" and I said, "Wow! And it's still working!" He chuckled as I realized what I had said. It is proudly displayed in our home and, yes, it is still ticking to this day.

Grandpa loved watching the kids play, going on little outings and feeding the ducks at the park. He was happy in our home and never complained. He was organized and liked his routine. He had half a grapefruit and two pieces of bacon every morning for breakfast; half a grilled cheese sandwich and four chips for lunch (if I gave him five, there would be one left over on his plate); and whatever I made for dinner was fine with him. He did this every day for two years. When I asked the doctor if it was okay for him to eat bacon every day, he laughed and said, "He's ninety years old—let him eat what he wants!"

We had fun together. Only God could bring a ninety-year-old man who could put up with our lifestyle. The kids always had friends over and we had people staying with us all the time, from all over the world. Grandpa loved to hear the missionaries' stories, and they would always leave with a generous contribution from a caring man who still had a part to play in God's work around the world.

As much as I loved Grandpa, I hated making his bed for him. Such a ridiculous complaint, but it was an inner fight every day. Then one day, as I was grumbling and yanking the covers up over his pillow, the Lord whispered into my ear, "Whatever you do for one of the least of My brothers, you do for Me." From that day forward, it was a joy and act of worship to make Grandpa's bed. God would meet me there—and He was to meet Grandpa there, too.

After two years, Grandpa's health began to deteriorate. He wanted to die at home. We discussed it as a family and agreed that it was God's will to give Grandpa the desire of his heart (an amazing act of grace from an eleven- and sixteen-year old). He was slipping fast, though his mind had been alert just two months before.

One day in early December, amid the busyness of Christmas preparations, I noticed he had sores on his body. I asked my friend Francie, who was a nurse, what I should do. She told me to sponge-bathe him with baby oil in the water. I had never bathed him before and was embarrassed and not sure how to bring it up. But when I asked him, he said he would appreciate it. After I bathed him, Grandpa looked into my eyes unashamedly and said, "Thank you."

How gracious was that man! Later the Lord showed me the Scripture, "She has done a beautiful thing to me. ... In pouring this ointment on my body, she has done it to prepare me for burial" (Matthew 26:10, ESV).

The next day Grandpa called me into his room and told me he was having hallucinations.

I asked him about it and he said, "I was at Cape Canaveral and they were doing the countdown."

I smiled and asked, "Grandpa, do you think the Lord is preparing you for takeoff?"

He closed his eyes and smiled.

I had tried sharing the gospel with him many times, but felt awkward in the words. So I called my friend Maria and she said, "He's a quiet man. God will meet him in a quiet way. You don't have to tell him the gospel; he has seen the gospel. When he reaches up his hand to you, he will be reaching out to Jesus."

A few days later Grandpa called me into his room again, complaining of hallucinations. I asked him what he saw this time and he said, "I see a man. He's calling out to me, but I can't hear him. He's a stranger and I can't hear what he's saying to me."

I said, "Grandpa, that's Jesus. He's calling your name."

Grandpa looked up at me and reached out his hand. We sat like that for thirty minutes in peaceful silence.

Three days later Grandpa Great died in his sleep. God had given him the desire of his heart. "Precious in the sight of the LORD is the death of his saints" (Psalm 116:15).

Keith had stayed home sick from school that day. We held each other and cried as they carried Grandpa's body out the door. I was so grateful Keith was there with me. There was comfort in sharing that moment together that I will never forget.

Friends came over to be with us and offered to clean the house for all the company and family who would be visiting. The house was a mess. It was December 12 and I had been working hard on Christmas gifts and ignoring dust and laundry and dishes. I was humiliated and hid in the bathroom for a good cry. Suddenly, I saw Grandpa's eyes looking into mine with gratitude after I had washed his body. He had cared

119

enough to put me at ease and had the humility to receive a humbling gift. Could I do any less? I went out and thanked my friends. Grandpa Great had taught me so much.

That night our friend Jeff called from Florida. He said he had been praying when the Lord gave him a word for us. He didn't know what it meant but knew he had to call right away. Then, before I even told him about Grandpa, Jeff repeated what he had heard in prayer: "Because you reached out with the hand of My love, we are no longer strangers and he is here with Me."

I love the Lord for the mercy He showed me that night so I could know Grandpa was with Him in heaven. He didn't have to tell me—that was between them—but I am ever grateful that He did.

And I am grateful that my husband, Loren, is carrying on the name of a quiet, gentle giant in the same manner for God's Kingdom. If you listen carefully, you can learn a lot from a quiet man.

AFRICAN TREASURES

Before he died, Grandpa handed me a check for a thousand dollars and told me it was for me—not for Loren, not for the kids, and not for the house, just for me!

What was left? I couldn't imagine what I could spend that much money on if it didn't involve any of my family or the house. I spent hours fretting over how to spend that money. It started to make me nervous. Finally I put it on my dresser with a prayer that I wouldn't touch it again until the Lord showed me why Grandpa had felt the need to give it to me.

The prayer was answered quickly. The very next day I received a phone call from my friend Betsey, inviting me to go with her and two other women to Kenya, East Africa. The purpose of the mission trip would be for teaching and praying with the women at a university in Nairobi and training them in godliness. I would be part of the prayer team. We would also take a day trip to a children's home in Nairobi. Betsey told me I would need to raise $1,200 in support. There it was! That must have been what the thousand dollars was for. I said yes right away.

You can't imagine how big this miracle was in my life. I had been afraid to become a Christian for this very reason. I was sure God was going to make me go to Africa ... or Texas.

121

(They were both big and far away.) Yet when the time came, I had no fear. God had transformed my heart.

The women and I met every week for months in preparation for the trip. We obtained our passports, shots and information about the people and country we would be visiting. We prayed for the women of Kenya and for ourselves. We were ready to have God use us, however He desired.

I knew the purpose of the trip was to minister mainly to the women of Kenya, but every time I prayed I envisioned the same thing. I saw myself holding a little boy in my arms and singing to him. It was always the same beautiful black face. He was one of the little ones at St. Nicholas Children's Home. We were supposed to make a side trip there just to love the kids and encourage the staff. I felt God would use me at the university, but this little boy was my true purpose in going to Africa.

I was excited when the day finally arrived for us to leave. Loren took me out for a nice, romantic breakfast. I was packed and ready to go. Our kids, my mother and sisters would be coming with Loren to see me off at the airport. This was a big moment in our lives; I had never been out of the country before.

Loren and I got home from the restaurant and found a message on the answering machine. The trip was canceled. The Persian Gulf War had broken out that day and we would not be allowed to fly. It broke my heart. I sat on the edge of my bed and cried as Loren held me. And then I started laughing. It struck me how remarkable it was that the Lord could change my heart so radically. My entire Christian life I had been afraid I would have to go to Africa, and now the hardest thing God had ever asked me to do was *not* to go to Africa, but to stay home with my family.

That evening, I just needed to be alone. I soaked in a warm bath, with tears streaming down my face. I pictured again that little boy cradled in my arms and sensed that I would never get to sing to him. As I prayed for him, the Holy Spirit whispered to my heart, "The important thing is not that you hold him, but that he be held." I prayed that someone else would hold him that very moment and sing to him the words Jesus wanted him to hear.

I believe with all my heart that it was done and I was released from the need to go.

God works in a mysterious way. Although I didn't go, I had been willing. Though He didn't use my arms, He used my heart; and through prayer, a child was comforted.

That could be the end of the story, but three years later I received another call inviting me to go to Kenya. The purpose of this mission trip was to spend ten days with the children in the care of St. Nicholas Children's Home. Now, instead of going for half a day, we would be there for ten days; and instead of going for one child, I would be going to minister to ninety-nine children. God had taken the seed of willingness and multiplied it a hundred times over. God wasn't making me go to Africa; He was letting me go.

Grandpa's money was long gone, but God provided yet again in wonderful and miraculous ways. The Bonner children from my Sunday school class washed the car, raked leaves and did other chores around their house in order to send me to Africa with a total of $11.34. Like the loaves and the fish, God multiplied their generosity.

Our Shepherd Group (a wonderful gathering of close-knit friends from different churches and denominations who met weekly to worship the Lord and study the Bible together) supported me financially and prayerfully. And, perhaps most precious to my heart, my mother also supported me. She had not wanted me to go, so her support was also her blessing.

The experience humbled me. I brought my guitar with me on the plane and, once there, led worship at St. Nicholas. Those kids knew how to praise God long before we arrived. They loved to sing and dance before the Lord. We presented a Vacation Bible School lesson each day, with music, prayer, puppet shows, skits, teaching and sharing.

My favorite part of the whole trip was simply hanging out with the children. They ranged in age from four to eighteen. One little boy had a smile that spread from ear to ear. Even his eyes smiled, which made his story all the more precious. His parents had both died and he had been living on the dangerous streets of Nairobi, when he was hit by a bus and left on the side of the road to die. A compassionate couple found him and brought him to St. Nicholas. The entire left side of his body was a continuous and deep scar, and he walked with a severe limp, but he was the happiest child I have ever met. He was kind and watched out for the little ones.

The children lived in small buildings lined with rows of bunk beds. They had a chapel, dining room, and a large room for activities. There was a field for playing soccer or other games, as well as large fields for growing much of their own food. They owned two milking cows. The older children helped with the younger ones and everyone had daily chores for which they were responsible.

The first few days we were there, we had no running water. We took a "shower" with a cup and bucket of cold water. Then one day, to our surprise, there was running water—literally! The water truck had arrived, and one of the teenagers would *run* to the water, fill a bucket and pour it into the container on the roof above the shower. What an expression of love!

The mission team also went to people in the community. We traveled to the small home of a couple out in the country on a rugged dirt path. That path was the darkest place I have ever seen on the face of the earth, and the stars were brilliant and impossible to count. It was as if we were standing in the middle of the Milky Way. It was breathtakingly beautiful. I was reminded once again of the night I sat in the hot tub on the mountain resort and heard God's promise of blessing in my life. This was surely one of them.

The home of this couple was handmade from pieces of aluminum and actually resembled a shed. Our new friends presented us with a feast of food and fellowship. We shared stories about what the Lord was doing in our lives and in our countries. We sang, "jumped" (a kind of dance) and laughed until the wee hours of the morning. I forgot we were in Africa; we were just visiting family.

Back at St. Nicholas, it seemed their favorite activity involved the button maker we had brought with us. It gave them something with their own name imprinted on it, bestowing each a sense of individuality and identity. My button said "Mama Keith" because women are called by the name of their firstborn child. One day we went to an open-air market (a very different experience for me), and I had forgotten to take off my button. As I was walking down the row of stalls, someone kept yelling, "Mama Keith, Mama Keith, I have such a deal for you."

One day, as I was sitting outside with a group of teenage girls, one of them suddenly pulled some hair out of my head. She was amazed at how different our hair felt. I was more amazed at how similar we were. We all have the same needs— to love and be loved, to touch and to feel, to be accepted for who we are, and to know the Creator who made us all. We need to know that God has a future and a hope planned for each of us. We need to know Jesus.

Each day, the children ate the same thing for dinner—a strong green vegetable and a white starchy substance. (I have long since forgotten the names of these foods.) One night a child prayed before the meal, "Father, thank You for this food, and we ask that You bless it. Please be with those less fortunate than ourselves." I was deeply touched. I had thought they had so little—no parents, no home of their own, just a bed and a little food. But I was so wrong. They had faith, they had each other and they had people who cared and were providing for their basic needs. More than that, they had the promise of God that He would be a Father to the fatherless; and He had been faithful. They were rich in the eyes of God because they had full and grateful hearts.

The day before we left, they held a feast in our honor. In that way they were giving honor to the God who had sent us. We all serve the same merciful Father.

The children, the staff and friends from the community were all there. They dressed in their native costumes and danced for us. They sang "He Walked Where I Walk," their favorite song we had learned together, using a native drum rather than my guitar. They killed one of their two cows so we could have meat. It was humbling, and their generosity was overwhelming. I'll never forget the children's faces lining the driveway, waving and crying as we left to return home. I was crying right along with them. My life would never be the same.

No, I never saw the face of the little boy I was to hold three years earlier. Instead I saw the face of Jesus expressed in ninety-nine different ways. Together, we make up the beautiful Body of Christ.

THERE'S ROOM AT THE INN

While I was in Africa, Loren and the kids attended summer camp with others from our church. I came home and excitedly shared stories and pictures of beautiful children with broad smiles and brightly shining eyes. Loren also shared pictures of beautiful children with broad smiles and brightly shining eyes.

Two young girls in particular stood out in Loren's mind. He described how they participated in everything with enthusiasm. They practiced every day with the worship dance group and then performed the dance on the last evening of camp. Along with all the children there, they truly entered into a place of worship. It was obvious to me that they had touched Loren's heart deeply.

The excitement of the summer passed quickly and the reality of life hit hard. Keith was leaving for college.

Actually, I was amazed at how well I took it. It was harder to let him get on the bus for kindergarten than it was to watch him drive off to college. But the truth is, I was in denial and pretended that he was just spending the night at a friend's house. Two months later we were moving Cheryl into his room when I completely fell apart. We were breaking down "the shrine." I hadn't changed a thing in his room since he left, and felt every emotion a mother can feel.

No, things would never be the same—nor were they supposed to be. Children are entrusted to our care by God. We don't own them; they belong to their Father. We are to raise them and prepare them to leave and become responsible adults. It's never easy to let go, but knowing the Lord will *never* let them go has to come by faith. Keith was in good hands. Besides, our role as parents wasn't over; it was just changing.

The reason Cheryl was moving into Keith's room was twofold. One, it's the rite of passage for the second child, and two, our family was growing.

There had been an announcement at church that a father was seeking a family to take his daughters into their home while he received treatment in an alcohol rehabilitation center. They lived in a motel near the church. We didn't know who they were, but our hearts were filled with joy when the door opened to the beautiful smiling faces of Ceamone and Lakea, the girls from summer camp! Their fear melted away when they saw Loren and Cheryl. They had all become friends at camp and were comforted by the fact that they wouldn't be living with strangers after all.

I remember the first night they stayed with us. They helped me by setting the table. They loved my cooking, which endeared them to me for life. I asked them what time they went to bed and Lakea said 9:00 until Ceamone nudged her and she changed her answer to 9:30. At 9:30 sharp I sent them off to bed, and overheard Lakea whisper to Ceamone, "I like it when things match." I realized then that I had made a point to have our dishes match when they didn't even have dishes.

What a blessing it was to have them in our home! I saw our life through their eyes and was suddenly grateful for the "little things" I took for granted, like matching dishes and a dishwasher to clean them.

Every night I sent them to bed at 9:30 and every night they were up until after midnight. I finally asked them why they were having trouble sleeping and they admitted that they always stayed up that late. When I asked them why they had told me their bedtime was 9:30, they said that if I asked that question, then it must be "normal" to have a bedtime, so they made one up. We kept the 9:30 bedtime.

We had a basement full of games, and I discovered, years later, that they had made a secret pact to play every game at least once before they left. Somehow, they were able to accomplish this incredible feat.

The girls were wonderful. They did well in school, played sports, joined the worship dance team and became Sunday school teachers. Cheryl finally had sisters, and we truly became a family. The girls called us their "godparents." They lived with us for six months, and during the last two months, their father and brother also moved in with us. Their father became a very dear lifelong friend. I'm glad there was room at the inn when God knocked on our door in the form of this family. It was a wonderful, chaotic, crowded home full of laughter and love.

Every night for six months, I tucked the girls in, kissed their cheeks and whispered the same thing I told Keith and Cheryl every night of their lives, "Goodnight. I love you and Jesus loves you." It was their favorite time of the day (though they never quite got the hang of a 9:30 bedtime), and they said they would always keep that ritual with their own children when they grew up.

They grew up faster than intended. They both gave birth to babies while in their teens. It broke my heart and filled it to overflowing at the same time. I had the privilege of being in the delivery room when Robert was born to Lakea by Cesarean section and then again when poking my head around the curtain to see Nyjsha come into this world and being laid into the waiting arms of Ceamone. I have seen the struggles of single parenting and know there are consequences for the choices they made, but they absolutely know that Jesus still loves them and their children, and we do, too. Now, many years later, we are "grand-godparents" to eight beautiful children whom we dearly love.

One Sunday before Christmas, we met Ceamone and her family at their church to watch the children offer their gifts of song and mime to the Lord. As she hugged us goodbye, she said, "Thanks for everything, Mr. and Mrs. Nystrom." Loren replied tenderly, "You know, Ceamone, I think you're old enough to call us by our names now." She responded immediately, "You mean like 'Dad'? That's how I've always felt about you."

Psalm 68:6 tells us that "God sets the lonely in families." We now have the honor of being "Mom and Dad" to Ceamone, not out of disrespect for her own parents, but out of awe and acceptance that we are part of a bigger family, one knit together by God's love.

YOUNG LOVE

When we allow God to have control, our lives become intertwined with many interesting people throughout our short walks on earth. I often worried that we had somehow robbed our own children of time and attention by opening our home to others. But as adults, Keith and Cheryl both assured us that their lives had been enriched by those encounters. They knew our hearts and shared our passion for helping those in need.

We were once asked to share our home with a teenage girl whose mother suffered with mental illness. This mom showed up at church one Sunday and started screaming at me at the top of her lungs in front of everyone standing in the lobby. People thought I was a saint for the calm way I handled the matter. Truthfully, she was yelling in Spanish and I didn't understand a word she was saying. That made it easy for me not to get my feelings hurt.

Due to her illness, this single mother needed temporary help raising her children. They really loved their mother, and we actually became friends with her once she learned to trust us.

During her time with us, Delia celebrated her quinceañera

(fifteenth birthday) with a grand party in our home. She looked like a princess and said she felt loved and honored. She joined us on our family vacation and was active in the life of our church. She became a member of the youth group and joined Cheryl at summer camp and retreats.

She had a boyfriend, but social services would not permit them to date, for good reason: Juan was a member of a gang. They were finding ways to be together anyway, so with the permission of the authorities, I invited him to come over for lunch so I could chaperone their time together. Delia was excited and made all her favorite Latino foods to impress him, and it worked. We were about to drive him home when her social worker arrived an hour early to take Delia to an appointment.

I felt uncomfortable being left alone with Juan. While I was standing in the kitchen, he came in and appeared to block the doorway with his arms. I prayed for God's peace and protection. Then, unexpectedly, he asked, "Do you really know Jesus?" And he covered his face and wept.

We sat together on the sofa as he grieved the death of his best friend in a gang-related shooting. Juan had witnessed this murder, and the lasting pain he endured was tangible. He wanted out of the gang but didn't know what to do. Despite my preconceived notion and fear, I discovered a young man reaching out for hope, compassion and a better life. I was ill-prepared to understand his circumstances but shared what I did have—hope and faith in the One who came to release us from the bondages of this world. I had the great privilege of praying with Juan that afternoon to receive God's mercy, forgiveness and grace as he asked Jesus into his life.

Delia stayed with us for about nine months. Then she and Juan broke up and she went back to live with her mother. Our family eventually lost contact with all of them.

Many years later, Loren and I were out on a date, stopping by a favorite spot at a shopping complex with a huge fountain in the courtyard. It sprayed streams of water straight up into the air at random times, to the delight of the children running through it. Loren and I loved to watch the sheer joy on the unsuspecting faces of the children and hear the laughter of their parents.

On this particular night, I noticed a young couple on the other side of the fountain. The woman was nestled up against her boyfriend with her back to him, leaning her head against his chest. He had his arms wrapped tightly around her, and I thought to myself, *Ahh, young love.*

Just then they laughed, grabbed each other's hands and made a run for it through the fountain. Out of the corner of my eye, I recognized him.

"Juan," I exclaimed, "is that you?"

Surprised, he turned around, grabbed me, lifted me off my feet and swung me around. "Sue Nystrom, I can't believe it's you. I never forgot you; you're an important part of my testimony." Then he reached into his pocket and pulled out the keychain I had given him fourteen years earlier, engraved with the words, "For the LORD your God will be with you wherever you go" (Joshua 1:9).

The four of us went out to dinner that night, and Loren and I learned that Juan's life had gotten worse before it got better. He spent quite a bit of time in jail. But Jesus never forgot the call He had on this young man's life, and He never let go.

With Jesus as his Redeemer and the help of others along the way, Juan is now a faithful servant of Christ. He was baptized and joined a local church. He went on to get a college diploma and is now working his way through medical school.

133

He is a motivational speaker for justice and the prevention of youth violence. He speaks with authority as one who has lived it—and lived beyond it.

At the end of our conversation that evening, I mentioned to Juan and his girlfriend how much their "young love" had touched my heart. Her eyes grew wide and moist as she said, "Believe it or not, I noticed you and Loren holding hands across the fountain and thanked the Lord for 'old love.'"

Loren and I laughed. We always smile when we see a cute elderly couple walking together hand in hand, but it was a shock to realize that we were the cute old couple!

She explained that her parents were going through a divorce and she was skittish about entering a relationship with no guarantee for the future. So she had prayed that God would bring a couple into her life who had been happily married for at least twenty years. To her astonishment, we doubled her criteria. More than that, we knew the One whose love endures forever.

Loren and I stand amazed, along with our children, at how God has enriched our lives with the interesting people we have met along the way. He doesn't ask us to save the world; only He can do that. But if we are obedient to do our small part, He can multiply those efforts and bring change into the lives of countless others.

Psalm 100:5 proclaims this truth: "For the LORD is good and his love endures forever; his faithfulness continues through all generations."

I REMEMBER...

It's funny how childhood experiences echo so loudly in adult life. I remember, for instance, that when we were young and our parents went out, our brother, Rich, was always our babysitter. Mom would inevitably give him chores to do around the house while they were gone. Rich was brilliant. As soon our parents left, he would invite us to play "Sergeant." My sisters and I loved this game! Rich would call us to "Atten...*tion*!" and Diane, Janice, Joanne and I would fall into line with a salute worthy of the commander-in-chief.

He would bark out orders like "Make my bed. Do the dishes. Scrub the bathroom. Dis...*missed*!" And off we would race to finish our assignments as quickly as possible in hopes that there would be others to follow.

I don't think the reason we liked the game was so much because we were stupid as it was that we were honored that our older brother would play with us. But here's the irony: Rich grew up to be a sergeant in the Army. I'm sure the men under him loved it as much as we did.

Another fond memory is a game I created for my sisters. Come to think of it, it was probably much the same for them as playing "Sergeant." I would come home from Catholic school each day, put a gray wool skirt with an elastic waistband on my head (hence becoming a nun), line my sisters up at their "desks" and play "School." I even gave them exams, and possessed my own inkpad with happy-faced and sad-faced angel stamps for grading their papers.

I think they put up with me because they were honored that their older sister would play with them.

I loved school as a child. My favorite toy was a nun doll my parents had given me for Christmas one year. My best memories were from second and seventh grades because of the love the nuns had shown me during those two years.

Now here's an irony my husband uncovered: Though I never became a nun, I taught *second grade* Sunday school for ten years before I went on to become a junior high youth pastor, teaching *seventh-* and eighth-graders. My heart had been moved and prepared to duplicate and spread the love and understanding I had received during those two vital years of my youth.

I loved teaching and seeing the minds and hearts of His little ones come alive as they understood a new truth. I wholeheartedly agree with St. John when he says, "I have no greater joy than to hear that my children are walking in the truth" (3 John 4). Teaching children is a privilege.

In my mind's eye, I can still see a little boy in second grade Sunday school coming up to me after class asking for prayer. I knelt down (he was so small) so I could lay hands on him as we prayed. Years later, as a senior in high school, he once again came to me for prayer. He knelt down (I was so small) so I could lay hands on him as we prayed.

It has been such an honor to be part of children's lives and watch them grow up to become godly men and women. We have a history together and a deep respect for one another.

Every young person who walked through those church doors holds a treasured place in my heart. The memories are enough to last a lifetime. Here are just a few:

I remember the night we were on retreat and one of the boys who was somewhat of a social outcast ran up and told us, "This is the best night of my life! No one has ever shouted my name before!" (We were playing a game and the kids on his team were chanting his name and cheering him on.) I also celebrated the night he heard Jesus call his name as he accepted Him as the Lord in his life.

I remember the night I let kids smash eggs on my head, at five dollars a pop, as a fundraiser to send one of the girls on a mission trip to Costa Rica.

I remember watching a young man conquer his fear as he crossed a log thirty feet in the air on a high ropes course, then observing that newfound confidence change his life in the years that followed.

I remember taking thirty-two kids to an amusement park while I was suffering with two sprained ankles and had to be pushed around in a wheelchair. As we split off into groups, I was sure none of the kids would want me because I would slow them down. But they surprised me when they fought to have me in their groups instead. Pride filled my heart as I thought I had a small part to play in teaching them compassion for those in need. Turns out you can move to the front of the line if you have someone with you in a wheelchair. Oh well …

I remember eating a lot of pizza and being supplied affectionately with my favorite breath mints—which continued long after I retired.

I remember a retreat in which there was an incident involving some of the boys. I didn't know who was caught up in it, but I pleaded with them to see me privately so things could be set right. Before we left the retreat center the next day, one boy came to me and wiped away the tears as he confessed his involvement. He couldn't live with the guilt of his secret. I was proud of his honesty and purity of heart. He became a man in my eyes that day.

I remember spending the night at the hospital when one young teen tried to commit suicide. How thankful I was years later as I sat in the church, watching her walk down the aisle toward the man waiting to call her his wife.

I remember one young man who came into youth group, sat down with his arms folded defiantly across his chest and announced the only reason he was there was that his mother made him come. He didn't scare me. In fact, I rejoiced in his transformation as he became a leader and actually led a whole night of youth group, from beginning to end, on his own.

I remember the night the Holy Spirit threw out my plans for the evening and how the kids spent the entire night in prayer and intercession for Columbine High School and the kids in their own schools.

I remember two beautiful girls dancing before the Lord to the song "Sincerely Yours" and meaning it with all their hearts.

I remember the retreat when the adult prayer team stepped back because God had moved the kids to minister to each other instead. Some were praying, some were singing and some were offering tissues to those in tears. I was so grateful for the privilege of seeing kids in worship of their Savior that night.

I remember giving each youth a nondescript picture that they were to stare at for thirty seconds, then close their eyes. Just as if it were yesterday, I can see the looks on their precious faces as the face of Jesus appeared behind their closed eyes. I'd seen that look before as the Jesus of their Bibles became Lord of their lives. How can anyone describe the immeasurable joy of salvation?

I remember creating a scavenger hunt in the form of a murder mystery. The kids had to decipher clues that led them to the victim (the Messiah, found on a poster at a store advertising a play); the weapon (a nail in the sign for *Nails* at a beauty salon); the motive (John 3:16, written on a card and distributed by a policeman manning the Crime Solvers window at the precinct). The last clue revealed the great price paid for such a crime. The youth were taken to a dollar store. When they went to the counter with their purchase, the cashier announced, "The price is paid in full—it's free." I paid the owners of the store in advance, just as Jesus paid our debt in full. Salvation is free to all those who will receive it. It was an interactive lesson on the death of Christ and His extreme love for us.

I remember a boy riding a unicycle while juggling for our talent show.

I remember the first night one seventh-grader came to youth group. She hung around afterward and told me that her family hadn't eaten in three days. I took her mother grocery shopping the next day and then sat with the girl as she showed me her family album. It was full of bulletins from the funerals of many in her family murdered during drug deals gone bad. I felt so small as I realized how different our worlds were and that there was little I could do to help. It was God's job to protect and redeem; it was my job to love and obey.

I remember loving every moment of teaching and sharing God's Word.

I remember learning more from the kids than I ever taught.

I remember with affection and gratitude all the leaders who sacrificed their time and talents to help me carry on this ministry.

I remember the letters I received telling me how God had changed the lives of those precious youth through teachings and unconditional love.

I remember with fondness the promise of a young man to take me into his home and care for me when I'm old and feeble and unable to feed myself. I repeated this pledge to him and his wife at their wedding. My bags are packed; I'm sure she won't mind.

I remember students sitting around a pond at sunrise in total silence, waiting with journals and hearts open to hear what God might speak to them.

I remember sitting around a campfire as a young girl released the hatred she held in her heart against the man who had murdered her brother, and the sense of freedom and peace that filled the air after her surrender to the Lord. The owners of the retreat center said they had never seen such power pour forth from believing teens as the kids surrounded her in encouragement and prayer.

I remember our annual tournament of Winnie the Pooh's favorite game, "Pooh-Sticks." It was amazing to see really cool teenagers scouring the land for the perfect stick and then lining up on the covered bridge to drop it into the water and rush to the other side to see whose stick would appear first. There was always great anticipation over winning the coveted "fabulous prize." Some of life's most simple pleasures bring with them our most treasured memories.

I remember all these—and more.

I remember the day I got the call asking me to consider taking the position of junior high youth pastor, and I remember the day God called me to lay it down. It was His to give and His to take back to pass on to someone else. Their new youth pastor told me graciously that it would be hard to fill my shoes.

I told her I was taking my shoes with me. If God wanted the same old thing, He would have left me there. He was going to do something new and He was going to do it through her.

I am grateful for these memories and hundreds of others I hold dear and ponder in my heart. I still pray for the "kids," many now with families of their own, but I am happy and content that I finished what God asked me to do, and I pray that our time together will continue to bear fruit. I look forward to seeing the harvest in the future.

"Train a child in the way he should go, and when he is old he will not turn from it" (Proverbs 22:6).

I look now to the Captain of the heavenly army in hopes that more assignments will follow. He's got my full Atten...*tion*!

HIS RESTING PLACE

There was to be no new assignment for the moment. What an empty feeling! I knew that the Lord had called me to a year of rest, but what does that mean? What does it look like? I had been excited about the possibilities—until the day I woke up with nothing to do. I found myself wandering the aisles of a local store.

I was standing in the greeting card section when I was struck with an overwhelming sense of identity loss. It physically hurt. I dropped my hands to my side and, in desperation, spoke these words out loud: "What now, Lord?"

My eyes fell on a Hallmark™ card on the rack. Out of curiosity, I picked it up and read, *"Come away with me, my love; the winter is past, the rain is over and gone. The flowers appear on the earth, and their fragrance fills the land. Come away with me."* I could feel His presence with me. Jesus had heard my sighing. I opened the card and found this invitation: *"Let's take some time to just enjoy each other ... to just be in love."*

That's what this year of rest was all about. I never felt more loved than at that very moment, and I knew He would teach me how to love Him more fully in return.

I read that card over and over again. Then I bought it and tucked it away in my Bible, where I could be reminded of His tender voice every day.

I enjoyed a year filled with rediscovering my love for Jesus and His love for me. It was filled with quiet walks by the water, Bible study, enriched prayer times, naps, exercise, spending time with friends, traveling and enjoying His amazing creation; silent times to remember, awareness to truly live in the present, acceptance that the future for now was to be silent. It was a precious gift of time in which my eyes were wide open to see Him and my heart fully open to feel and experience His presence in the everyday.

In Hebrews 4:11 (ESV), Scripture tells us to "strive to enter that rest." It had always seemed odd that *strive* and *rest* should appear in the same sentence. Now I understood. Resting is hard work. I had to fight many times to keep peace. It's hard to give yourself permission to say no to people wanting to put you in charge of things. It's hard to explain why you're not working and what you do with your time. Most people do not approve. It's hard not to feel lazy or guilty when you see things that need to be done and know you're capable of doing them.

There is a saying I learned to embrace: "The stops of a man are ordered by the Lord as well as His steps." We are willing to do great things for Christ, but are we willing to do nothing? Sometimes God says, "Stop," and if we keep going, it's called disobedience. It doesn't feel natural to stop. I found rest to be supernatural.

That year, then, was a time to be quiet, to be happy, to be pampered and to reflect. It was glorious!

Sounds perfect, doesn't it? But I also discovered that life didn't stop around me just because I was resting. Most of it was wonderful, but it was peppered with deaths in the family, sickness, a flood and major home repairs, my best friend moving away and family members in need of help. Real life happened. The beauty in it all was that I was available. My hours weren't filled with busyness. I could be fully there for those who needed me. And when everything seemed to happen all at once, and I started to feel the world cave in around me, I knew where to run. I knew that the Lord is my refuge. I found peace deep within. I found, in the end, that it was well with my soul.

As that year came to a close, I found myself asking the Holy Spirit once again, "What now, Lord?" It was different this time—no desperation, no greeting card, just a pure and simple reply: "Do less, love more."

Years have passed since that first sabbatical, but His invitation remains the same: *"Let's take some time to just enjoy each other ... to just be in love."*

MUSIC TO MY EARS

When our children were younger, they participated in sports, and Loren and I would go from field to field to watch them play. When they became adults, we would go from bar to bar to *hear* them play. They are both musicians—very gifted and talented musicians.

I never thought the bar scene would be our mission field. I had never been to a bar before and, quite honestly, felt like an imposter; like Whoopi Goldberg in *Sister Act* when the customer said, "If this turns into a nun bar, I'm out of here." To my surprise, I loved it; or rather, I loved *them*. I felt an immediate connection with the people we met. They accepted us because we accepted them.

I remember Keith's very first show. His band was playing in a Mexican restaurant, and I really wanted to go but was afraid it would embarrass him. So Loren and I decided to go incognito. We ordered dinner like regular customers and pretended we didn't know him. To our delight, he brought his friends over to introduce us during a break. The next day one of his good friends said, "Do you know what Keith said was the best part of the show?" I guessed, "Hearing people applaud?" He replied, "No. It was looking up and seeing his parents there." And we've been there supporting Keith and

Cheryl ever since.

Keith has been in several bands over the years, but for quite some time he was in a band called Jack Potential. Their style of music was called "emo-metal," short for emotional metal. That just meant it was *loud*. Keith sang and, dare I say, there was melodic screaming. I had never heard anyone scream in tune before. He is an incredible songwriter and his voice is strong and quite beautiful. I always carried a six-pack—of earplugs, that is!—to every show and shared them with those around me. As his mother, I felt responsible. I never grew tired of people telling me how talented he was or that Keith was one of the nicest people they had ever met.

Cheryl picked up the guitar and wrote her first song at the age of twelve. I was sincerely moved because of the depth of the words and the melody that carried them. She had received a gift from God, and she continued to nurture and grow in that gift. She was a member of our worship and youth bands at church for many years, and was given the honor of writing her high school graduation song and performing it in front of two thousand people. She has been blessed to follow her passion ever since.

She and her partner, Jim Ball, formed a folk rock band called Mercy Creek and have been performing on the road for the last fifteen years. They are brilliant together. Cheryl's voice is beautiful, haunting and powerful. She is amazingly skillful on the guitar. Jim's body goes into warp speed during his drum solos. They are prolific and thoughtful songwriters and each album is unique, like the couple themselves. I love to eavesdrop as the crowd sings along or engages with them after every show. People are wowed and we are proud. What can I say? We are groupies. Cheryl truly is a beautiful woman, inside and out.

When my mother turned 70 (oops, I mean 39), my sisters and I went in together and bought her a boom box for her birthday. I also wanted to give her copies of our kids' CDs, so I went to the local music store to purchase them. When I asked the multi-pierced, multi-colored-spiky-haired kid working the floor if he could tell me where I could find a Jack Potential CD, he said he would have to check the computer. On the way, he inquired about the genre of music. When I said "emo-metal" (a term someone my age would not normally know), he paused with a curious look on his face. Back in motion, he couldn't stand it anymore and asked, very politely, "And will you be purchasing this CD for yourself?" I shot back, "No, it's for my mother." I thought he would pass out right there on the floor. It was hysterical. I let it hang in the air for a moment and then explained the whole story.

And then he shared his story with me. He was from California and was now bouncing from one friend's house to another because his parents had kicked him out of their home. They didn't approve of him joining a band and they didn't like his friends. He hadn't spoken to them in eight months. As I suspected, there was much more to the story. He opened up to me, honestly acknowledging all the other problems he was facing. In the end, he promised to call his parents when he got home that night. God is a reconciler and allowed me to be an unlikely insider for His greater purpose.

One night Loren and I were listening to Cheryl and Jim play at a bar when four men walked in and sat at a table across from us. As they watched them perform, we noticed that they were also watching us. Then two of the men came over and joined us at our table. The older gentleman asked if Cheryl was our daughter. Then he congratulated us and expressed his view about the importance of parental support. Their success would be sure and sweet, he believed, because we were there for them.

We talked for a long time when he suddenly blurted out to me, "I'm not coming on to you"—Loren was right there—"but I have to say that you are the most beautiful mother I have ever seen. There's something different about you."

"Thank you," I said simply. "It's Jesus."

"What?"

"I hope what you're seeing in me is Jesus."

He looked surprised, to say the least. He thought for a moment, and then asked what I did for a living. I told him I worked at a church and used to be a youth pastor.

"Then what are you doing in a bar?"

"Don't worry," I said, "it's not a conflict of interest. Jesus didn't spend all His time in churches or synagogues. Don't you think He'd be out where the people are who don't know Him yet?"

He looked stunned and laughed to himself. "Yeah, I guess He would." And with that he shook his head and went off to shoot pool.

A little later his friend returned and asked, "Do you really know God?"

I assured him that we did.

"I was brought up in a good Christian home," he confessed. "But I've gotten so far away that I don't know how to get back. Would you please pray for me?"

Right there in the middle of that dark bar, the man rededicated his life to Christ. He wouldn't go into a church, so God went into the bar.

Yes, God has blessed our children with beautiful voices and great musical ability. He has opened doors for ministry that Loren and I would never have found if not for them.

Cheryl and Jim continue to perform and profoundly touch the lives of people they meet along the way. They also provide 'round-the-clock care for Jim's mother, who is ill. As caregivers, they daily offer a sacrifice of love. They enjoy their cherished chickens, cats and Lilly, their albino dwarf rabbit. Cheryl has always loved animals. Proverbs 12:10 says, "The righteous care for the needs of their animals." This world needs more people with a heart as big as Cheryl's.

Keith no longer sings with a band. He and Loren now work together and share a strong father-son relationship. One of Keith's greatest desires was fulfilled last year when he married our beautiful daughter-in-law, Michelle, and became Daddy to two precious children. I wish someone would greet me the way these two light up when Keith gets home from work. CJ and Lexi have stolen our hearts and bring us much joy. When asked by his pediatrician what he wanted to be when he grew up, CJ thought for a moment and said, "I want to be a good man." I believe he is well on his way. And our precious Lexi is my baking companion and fashion advisor. I love our chats and her exuberance for life. Keith and Michelle are following God's plan for their family and their cup overflows with love.

These are the sounds that bring joy to my heart: the petitions of perfect strangers reaching out for God's mercy and love; the voice of our daughter on our weekly phone visits; the sound of our son praising the Lord alongside his family at church; and the laughter of grandchildren. This is music to my ears.

And I hope the echo of my constant refrain, "I love you and Jesus loves you," will always be music to their ears as well.

My heartfelt prayer is that they will one day hear the song

of the Almighty and sing it to an audience of One. He created them, He gifted them and He is their biggest fan.

"By day the LORD directs his love, at night his song is with me—a prayer to the God of my life" (Psalm 42:8).

SOMEBODY'S DAUGHTER

"I will lead you to those in the waste places." Those were the words spoken over me in 1987, when a small but mighty grandmother in the Lord came to prophesy over the women of our church. Through this godly woman, the Lord revealed that I have needed and received much grace in my life and that I am to extend that grace into the lives of others. He has infinite patience and doesn't give up on souls who have strayed. He is the Deliverer and He desires to set them free. He promised that "they will be born anew because they can read the chapters of grace and mercy and love when they have come to the place where they can read nothing else. And I will lead you to those in the waste places."

At the time, it frightened me to think of what that might mean. Where was God sending me? I have since discovered that it is not to a place at all; it is to a people. Where are these waste places? They can be found in the dramatic—on the streets with the homeless, with drug addicts and prostitutes. They can be found in the ordinary—at school, in bars, in our neighborhoods and in our churches. They can be found as far away as Africa and as close as my own soul. They are simply the broken places of the heart that can be repaired only by the

151

touch of God's grace.

It is easy to miss the opportunity to extend grace when we find ourselves in the place of judging others instead. I will never forget one morning after church, when our children were young, and we went to the donut shop for a special treat. We walked in and couldn't find a seat … unless you counted the several open seats creating a wide berth around a homeless man sitting there. He was wearing ragged clothes; we were wearing our church clothes. He smelled of living on the streets; we smelled of self-righteousness. The place was filled with others coming from church, yet not one person would be seen with him.

Until, that is, our son walked over and sat next to him. All eyes were on Keith, and we didn't move. He started talking to the man and asked him about all the stuff he had sitting on the counter, which included a book of matches, a penny and a dirty old rag. You could have heard a pin drop in that shop.

The man started sharing with Keith (and everyone else listening) that the matches were to remind him to be the light of Christ in a dark world. Every penny, he said, is a reminder of where we should place our hope; and he showed Keith the words *In God We Trust* on the coin. Then our son asked about the old rag. His new friend told him that he kept it so he would never forget what his heart looked like before God washed away his sins.

These are the lessons I learned from a boy and a street dweller. They were both evangelists spreading the grace of God in the waste places of those around them.

Years later I found another such place on the streets of Washington, D.C. Keith's band was playing in a bar just off 14th Street in the heart of the red light district. As Loren and I were driving to the show, we passed the first prostitutes I had ever seen in real life. I was shocked! There were girls lined up and down the street, barely dressed in what looked like underwear, while I gawked, mouth open, shaking my head. When we passed one girl, I turned to Loren and blurted out, "Did you see *that*?" Then I punched him in the arm for looking.

My ungracious comments on each girl continued until my eyes met the eyes of one of the young women—and then my heart broke. She was somebody's daughter and I was ashamed of my reaction.

As we drove on, I kept seeing her eyes looking back at me. I prayed for her then and prayed for her at the club. During a break, I told Keith about seeing her and the impact it had on my heart. Loren and I prayed for her before going to bed and prayed for her again when we woke up. I prayed for her and all the other girls on the street with a group from church the next morning and asked the Lord to send someone to minister to her. Then I heard His words once again: "I will lead you to those in the waste places."

She remained in my heart and prayers. Two weeks later, as the Lord directed, I sat down and wrote her a letter. That night, I asked Loren if we could go back to the streets and look for her.

We left home at ten o'clock one evening and drove to where we had last seen her, but the women were not at the same location. (It's not like you can ask a policeman for directions to the prostitutes.) So we kept driving around—no easy feat in D.C. Finally, at eleven o'clock, we found the street where they were working.

I searched the face of every girl but didn't see her, so we went around the block and looked again and again and again.

There we were, driving slowly down the street, looking at

prostitutes. Did I mention we drove an old Cadillac at the time? Nothing like being conspicuous! But I was sure God had said she would be there that night and I had to find her. Loren was so patient. We drove around the block for another fifty minutes until finally he said that was enough; it was time to go home. I begged for just once more (something I mastered as a child), and he agreed. One more time around the block and there she was, standing on the corner.

I jumped out before Loren even came to a complete stop, ran up to her and asked her perhaps the silliest question you can ask a woman of the streets: "Were you here two weeks ago?"

She looked at me, glanced apprehensively over at Loren in the car and said calmly, "No."

I laughed, assured her that she hadn't been with Loren, nor was that the reason we were there. I then said, "Let's start over again. I saw you here two weeks ago and I've been praying for you ever since. I have something for you. Please read it in a quiet spot."

She took the letter with a puzzled look and said cautiously, "Okay."

I turned to leave. Then I turned back, extended my hand and said, "By the way, my name is Sue."

She smiled, offered her hand to me and said, "Hi, my name is KiKi."

We shook hands. Something special transpired between us in that moment. Then I jumped back into the car and shouted, "Read it."

She held up the letter and turned back down the street.

This is what the letter said:

I don't know your name, but I can still see your eyes.

A few weeks ago, my husband and I were driving down 14th Street to see our son's band play at a club. It was the first time I had ever actually seen prostitutes on the street. I am ashamed to admit that my first response was morbid curiosity. I just stared with unbelief and kept making unkind remarks with each girl we passed, until my eyes caught yours. And my heart broke.

You were beautiful ... and sad. You were young and my heart was filled with just how much Jesus loves you. I couldn't get you out of my mind. I prayed for you. Your face stayed in my mind all night.

I belong to a prayer group at my church. I told them about you and we prayed together for you and all the other girls that we saw that night, but most especially for you.

I don't know what your story is. I don't know how you ended up on the streets. I don't know if you're on drugs, in trouble, a runaway, angry or scared. All I know is that I love Jesus and He loves both of us. All I want you to know is that someone cares and we're here to help and that God will show us how.

I am not judging you. I don't think I'm better than you. Obviously, I don't do the things that you do—our sins are just different.

The fact that you are reading this letter is proof that God answers prayers. I prayed that He would let me find you tonight. He will answer your prayers as well. Ask Him to help and He will show you the way out.

God's love is pure and our concern is genuine. Call when you are ready to reach out for true love—He loves you that much.

155

Then I signed my name and gave her our phone number.

I wish I knew the end of this story, but God doesn't always let us know all the details of someone else's life just because we had a small part to play in it. He called on me to plant a seed of hope and introduce her to His unconditional love. I trust Him completely to do the rest.

I told Keith that we found her and had given her the letter. He was playing again at the same bar the following week, so he shared the story with some friends there and it spread like wildfire. Some of the young people were impressed, but others were furious. What did we think we were doing? Did we honestly think that her pimp would just let her go and say, "It's okay—Jesus wants you?" Did we know how dangerous it was? And we gave her our phone number? Why would we risk our lives for a worthless prostitute? "Because Jesus did," was all I could say. The answer silenced them.

"If any one of you is without sin, let him be the first to throw a stone at her" (John 8:7). We are all unworthy, but not one of us is worthless. He paid a precious price to redeem us.

And Jesus asked, "Woman, where are [your accusers]? Has no one condemned you?" "No one, sir," she said. "Then neither do I condemn you," Jesus declared. "Go now and leave your life of sin" (verses 10–11).

We are all somebody's son, somebody's daughter. Mercifully, Jesus doesn't give up on us when we stray. He comes after us with a passion and takes us by the hand to lead us out of the waste places into the beautiful oasis of His extreme and extravagant love.

THE GOD OF ALL COMFORT

As I burst through the hospital room door, my mother opened her arms to receive my embrace and said, "Well, I guess you have another chapter for your book." I'd rather have her.

Keith had been trying frantically to reach us in Panama, to no avail. When Loren and I left for vacation, the doctors had assured us that she was fine. They even used the word *cured* after months of chemo treatments for lung cancer. But when our plane landed in Florida, my cell phone was ringing. Keith was choked up and told us we had better hurry home. He wasn't even sure we could make it in time.

How could this be happening? My mother was well when we left; how could she be dying now? I was desperate as we reached the ticket counter at the airport. The agent was working on changing our flight as soon as possible, but I was distraught; so she put her arm around me and said, "Honey, you need to put your trust in God."

We arrived at the hospital to an incredible scene. For the next seven days, 34 family members were camped out in the waiting room, all there to express their love and gratitude to the woman who had loved them with all her heart. Her children, grandchildren and great-grandchildren had gathered to be by her side. They came from as far away as Hawaii and Guam to be with her. Our father and Mom's friends joined us in the vigil. The doctor said, "Virginia, I already know you are an incredible woman because you have an incredible family. I have never seen love like this before."

Each of her children spent one night alone with her, and we have treasured memories that will remain with us forever. We also went in as family units to say goodbye. I will never forget standing in silent awe as Cheryl sang over her:

Rest easy and have no fear
I'll love you perfectly
At all times, my dear
I'll take your burden
And take your pain
So rest easy in My embrace

I went out to the waiting room and lay my head in my father's lap. He took his arthritic hand, with perfectly stiff fingers that hadn't been able to bend for years, and stroked my hair gently, assuring me that everything would be all right.

Even though Mom had been frustrated that she couldn't talk for the last two days, my sister Joanne realized it was because it was time for her to listen. Nothing had been left unsaid. We all knew how deeply she loved us, but now it was time for "her children [to] arise and call her blessed" (Proverbs 31:28). Mom was leaving a legacy of love.

The next morning we, her children, gathered around her bed. Rich was like a birthing coach as Mom entered her new life. Diane encouraged her to keep walking and not look back. Janice loved and released her from a job well done into the waiting arms of Jesus. Joanne held her hand and never let go. I prayed for one last miracle—that it would be done quickly and that she would be surprised by joy when she got there. We had the privilege of walking our mother to the doorstep of heaven.

And then she took her final breath.

At the funeral, my great-nephew Trevor looked into the casket and asked, "Why is Great-Nanny in that treasure chest?" Out of the mouth of babes! We will never again look into a casket without realizing the treasure it holds and give thanks for the life it represents.

Grieving is such a personal process. There is no right or wrong way to grieve. God will never rush us, but He walks with us until we are fully able to receive the comfort He alone can bring to our aching souls. I can't speak for the rest of my family, but this is how God brought me to that healing place:

It had been three months since my mother's death, and I was stuck in the same place of grief. I called out to the Lord for help, and He gave me His comfort in the form of a vision. I saw myself standing at the side of my mother's hospital bed, holding her hand and unable to let go. My husband and siblings were all there with me. I realized that it was the moment Mom took her final breath; always her final breath.

Then I saw Jesus standing in the doorway with His hand extended out to me. He said, "Come with Me; it's time to leave this place. She's not here anymore." I let go of Mom's hand and put my hand into His, never looking back as we walked through the doors into a beautiful sunlit garden. It was such a place of peace.

I knew in that moment that Mom was free from all the pain she had endured. And I was now in that place of freedom, too. I was free to cherish the memories and laugh again. The Lord had breathed new life into her. I could see her joyful in heaven with Jesus where she belonged. Her family was now called to continue her legacy of love.

Then, just eleven months later, my father passed away. One month after Mom died, Dad injured himself getting into the car, and he never quite recovered. He was a plasterer by trade and had suffered with asbestosis for years, but had refused to go to the doctor. Unlike my mother, it would have been torturous for Dad to be in the hospital for a week surrounded by family members. Instead, just two weeks before he died, all six of his children and many of his grandchildren gathered around to celebrate his 81st birthday. Dad was Irish, so a party, in hindsight, was God's gracious way of letting us say goodbye in a way Dad could receive.

The day before Dad died, I spent a nice day with him, sitting on his deck and chatting about all kinds of things. Later, we went back inside and he headed for his favorite recliner so we could talk some more. I had no idea he was dying, but I felt an urgency to thank him for something that had been on my heart for some time. It blessed him in a way I can't explain.

When it was time to leave, I ran up the stairs—but ran back down and blew him a kiss from the bottom step and said, "Love you!" and left. I am so thankful those were the final words he ever heard me say.

He had a bad cold, so my sister Diane came over and spent the night, just in case he needed her, as she had done so many times in the past. It was right that she be there. She had the privilege of sharing with him his last day on earth. They spent time reminiscing, and he left each of us a gift as he shared with Diane of his prayers for us individually.

For me, he said, "Maybe Jesus really does speak to her after all." We had many heartfelt conversations about prayer over the years. Knowing he believed me was like balm for my soul.

Then he told Diane, "My children know me and I know my children." He died in bed that very night.

When Janice told her son Pete (Dad's namesake) that Pop-Pop was in heaven, he said, "Well, the good news is he's with Nanny, and they're both with Jesus until we can all be together again."

The day of Dad's death, I went upstairs to find Aiden, Walter's son, playing with the "trouble stick," the name he affectionately gave Dad's walking cane (for obvious reasons). I asked him what he was doing, and he said, "Fishing—and I caught a big one!" It was a favorite pastime between him and his grandfather.

It's the same thing Jesus' disciples did after His death. In John 21:3 Peter said, "I am going fishing." The other disciples said, "We will go with you." Jesus appeared on the beach that day and ate with them. He met the disciples where they were; and He met me in the same way. Jesus has called us to be fishers of men. I found comfort "fishing" with Aiden that day.

On the evening of my father's death, I lay in bed, unable to find solace in sleep. I remembered Dad's hand bringing comfort the night before my mother died. I asked the Lord, "Who's going to comfort me now?"

His response was immediate and clear through the vision He set before me. Jesus and I were walking hand in hand through a lush, green field atop a cliff overlooking the ocean. Waves were crashing against the rocks below. Suddenly we stopped, and He sat down on a rustic bench. I sat at His feet and lay my head in His lap as He gently stroked my hair ... and I knew everything would be all right.

Isaiah 51:12 promises this everlasting truth: "I, even I, am He who comforts you."

A LOVE STORY

On June 17, 1972, at the tender age of nineteen, Loren and I stood solemnly before God, our family and each other and vowed, "To have and to hold, from this day forward, for better, for worse, for richer, for poorer, in sickness and in health, to love and to cherish, until death do us part."

Like everyone else who ever spoke those words, we had no idea what they meant. We can't see into the future; they were spoken as a promise, a commitment made by faith.

When we were only sixteen years old, Loren asked me if I would still love him when he was bald (his hair was longer than mine!), and I giggled and said yes, as long as he still loved me when I was fat (I weighed 92 pounds!). Both situations seemed ridiculous from the vantage point of youth. Years later, when my hair started falling out because of the medication I was on, I looked into the mirror, marched out to the living room and announced, "Okay, new scenario!" I trusted he would love me anyway; he had promised.

They say with age comes wisdom. It also brings great hindsight. We didn't know then what we know now, but we would both do it all over again.

To have and to hold – It's not so much to "own" but to truly "belong" to each other. We have held each other with

162

arms of love, wrapped in affection and intimacy meant only for the two of us. We have held each other up when we were about to fall. We hold each other back when we are heading for a mistake. We hold each other accountable and we hold each other in high esteem. We continue to hold each other in times of joy and sadness. God Himself joined us together and the two became one. We belong together.

From this day forward – Eleanor Roosevelt (and the wise turtle from *Kung Fu Panda*) once said, "Yesterday is history. Tomorrow is a mystery. Today is a gift. That's why it's called the present." Each day is a gift from the Lord. *I do* is present tense!

For better, for worse – This represents the ups and downs of life. It's the joy of becoming parents and holding our children for the very first time, and the agony of holding them through injuries, heartaches and rebellion, while still holding tenaciously onto God's promises for their lives. It's the times of feeling madly in love, and the times of exhaustion, frustration and miscommunication. It's the victories we have known in Jesus and the battles it took to get there. It is knowing that the "better" far outweighs the "worse."

For richer, for poorer – We've known both. There have been times we had plenty and times we had to go without. It is a blessing to have eyes to see that some of our poorest days were actually our richest because we saw the mighty hand of God move in miraculous ways on our behalf. Proverbs 30:8 says, "Give me neither poverty nor riches, but give me only my daily bread." Loren has worked hard to provide for his family through the years, and I am proud and respect him for that. I am content.

In sickness and in health – This is where Loren has perhaps most proven his love for me. I have suffered with poor health off and on for the last thirty years. I have experienced excruciating pain, a weak immune system and various rare diseases and complications. Loren has been steadfast through it all. He has stayed by my side and taken good care of me. He has taken off work to go with me to the doctor or to sit with me on hospital visits. During times of crisis, he has cleaned the house, cooked the meals and washed my hair. One time it looked like a comedy routine as he helped me get into my pantyhose (although why I thought I needed them to go to the hospital is beyond me!). He monitored my medications when it became overwhelming for me. He has made me laugh and let me cry. One night he carried me and lowered me gently into a warm bath for ten minutes out of every hour simply because it brought a little relief. More than anything, he has covered me in prayer, never giving up. He is my hero.

Perhaps because of all we have gone through, we truly appreciate our times of health. We enjoy life together and have discovered that we make great travel companions. We are on a quest to do one big thing in every state. We feasted our eyes on the Grand Canyon. We stumbled upon 600,000 motorcycles in Sturgis, South Dakota. We ate the best cherries ever on the way to exploring Michigan's Upper Peninsula. We have just returned from the trip of a lifetime to Alaska, where we felt like privileged children of God, experiencing His good pleasure in the beauty and majesty of that place. We even landed in a helicopter on a glacier and went dogsledding! We saw a moose in Maine and whales off Cape Cod. Life is a wonderful adventure.

To love and to cherish – It means to hold dear and treasure all we have been given in our life together as husband and wife. I love Loren with all my heart and know that I am loved. That's what we promised in 1972 and what we will continue to give each other today, tomorrow and every day until death do us part. Speaking of which …

Until death do us part – One night that pronouncement came a little early. We love to watch meteor showers and had driven away from the city lights to enjoy the show. I stared up into the night sky while Loren slept in the car. Around 2:30 in the morning, the meteors started shooting across the sky in a brilliant display. I woke him up and we relaxed on the hood of the car in absolute wonder. When I got chilly, he wrapped me up in a blanket. One lone car drove by. I looked over at Loren and said, "Isn't it amazing that we still enjoy doing this after all our years together?"

Just then a police car drove up beside us. I sat up and asked the policeman if he had been enjoying the meteor shower. "I thought so," he responded. I asked him what he meant. "Do you know why I'm here?" he asked. "I'm here because I got a report of a dead body on the hood of a car!"

The driver of that lone car must have seen Loren wrapping me up and thought he was disposing of the evidence!

I am truly thankful for every day the Lord has prepared for me on this earth, and I want to use each one to bring Him glory.

I know this is not everyone's story, but it is our love story and I thank God for the gift He has given us through each other. I have been blessed to be married to my very best friend for more than forty years. He is smart, funny and puts up with my plans and schemes. He worships God and loves his family. We grew up together and, by God's grace, we will grow old together.

My sister Janice was only fourteen years old when Loren and I married, but God used her heart in a powerful way to prepare us for our life together as husband and wife. On

165

Christmas Eve, the night of our engagement, Janice knelt through the entire midnight Mass interceding for us and asking God to bless our marriage and to make it last. To this day, she celebrates our anniversary with a prayer of thanksgiving that God honored her prayer.

I believe this love we share gives us an earthly glimpse into things yet to come. We await that glorious day Jesus Himself has been longing to celebrate. As hard as it is to fathom, we are being prepared as a Bride for her Bridegroom. We are the object of His affection and God the Father has promised our hand In marrlage to HIs beloved Son. He has called us to be the Bride of Christ—and you really can't do better than that!

Hallelujah!
For our Lord God Almighty reigns.
Let us rejoice and be glad
and give him glory!
For the wedding of the Lamb has come,
and his bride has made herself ready.
Revelation 19:6–7

EPILOGUE

Dear fellow traveler,

We all have a story to tell. *Your* life in *His* hand is very precious. It is a relationship filled with faith, hope and love.

If you don't yet know God as Father, take this moment to invite Jesus into your heart. He will forgive you, save you and fill you with new life. You are the reason He came and He loves you. You don't need to fix yourself to be worthy. He will take you as you are and then heal and restore your broken places. What a story you will have to tell!

If you are a child of God, then you already know that He loves you personally, passionately and perfectly. But you may be looking into your life and thinking there's nothing to tell. You may feel that your life is boring or difficult and that you haven't seen the victory people would be interested in hearing. Then share the battle, remembering that hope makes it bearable. People need to know that God is with them in those hard times in life. Ask God to open your eyes and heart as He reveals Himself in the ordinary moments of your day. They don't stay ordinary for long in His presence.

2 Chronicles 19:7 tells us that "with the LORD our God there is no injustice or partiality." God just doesn't have favorites! You are the one He loves; so are they. Your story may be the voice God uses to bring life to another person.

I hope you will be blessed on your unique journey and that one day we will meet along the way. I need to hear what you have to say.

"Then I heard the voice of the LORD saying, 'Whom shall I send? And who will go for us?' And I said, 'Here am I. Send me!' He said, 'Go and tell ...'" (Isaiah 6:8–9)

Made in the USA
Charleston, SC
08 September 2014